SURREY

ORDNANCE SURVEY HISTORICAL GUIDES

SURREY

Dennis Turner

GEORGE PHILIP

ORDNANCE SURVEY

First published in Great Britain in 1988 by George Philip & Son Ltd,
27A Floral Street,
London   WC2E 9DP
and Ordnance Survey,
Romsey Road,
Southampton SO9 4DH

Copyright © The maps in this publication are reproduced from Ordnance Survey maps with the permission of the Controller of HMSO. Crown copyright reserved, 1988

Text copyright © Dennis Turner 1988

British Library Cataloguing in Publication Data
Turner, Dennis
    Surrey.—(Ordnance survey historic county guides).
    1. Surrey—Historical geography
    I. Title   II. Series
    911'.4221   DA670.S96
ISBN 0-540-01135-5

Filmset by Tameside Filmsetting Ltd.
Ashton-under-Lyne, Lancashire
Printed by BAS Printers Ltd.
Over Wallop, Hampshire
Bound by Robert Hartnoll Ltd
Bodmin, Cornwall

Picture acknowledgements

The Francis Frith Collection: pp 54, 100–101, 120–121
Alan Ingram and Malcom Pendrill: pp 94–95, 97, 99
Kingston upon Thames Corporation, Heritage Centre: pp 43, 52–53
London Borough of Croydon: pp 58–59, 106–107
London Borough of Sutton Libraries, Local Collection: pp 61, 64–65
London Transport Museum: p 34
Merton Library Service: p 62
Malcom Pendrill: 33 (top), 35, 45, 49, 55, 60, 61 (top), 63, 67, 68, 71 (lower), 79, 82, 83, 86 (lower), 96, 110, 114, 115, 116, 119
Radio Times Hulton Picture Library: endpapers, pp 1, 2, 7, 11, 23, 27, 33 (lower), 37, 38–39, 46, 48, 62, 90

Endpapers: *Kew Bridge in the late nineteenth century.*

Half-title: *A fête given by the Duke of Buccleugh for Queen Victoria at his villa in Richmond in the 1840s.*

Frontispiece: *Bell Street, Reigate, with the Bell Inn itself on the left.*

Contents

———◇◇◇———

Surrey

Drawn & Engraved by C.Rosenberg

SURREY CRICKET GROUND.

Surrey Cricket Ground in 1846, shortly after its completion.

THE COUNTY OF THIS BOOK is the county as it existed before the London Government Act of 1889. It occupied a rough rectangle of 200,000 ha (750 square miles) with London at its north-east corner and Windsor just beyond its north-west. It measured rather under 65 km (40 miles) in its greatest extent from east to west and 32–42 km (20–26 miles) from north to south. It was thus about four times the size of Rutland and one-eighth the size of Yorkshire. The Thames formed a natural boundary on its north but, apart from one eight-mile stretch on the west where the Blackwater formed its boundary, the county had no other natural boundary.

Although one of the smaller English counties, Surrey has not one landscape but a mosaic of several—the still well wooded Weald; the wild, rough sweeps of the Greensand with the heathland around Hindhead and Leith Hill; the more desolate heathland in the north-west of the county; the chalk upland of the North Downs; the overbuilt landscape of the Thames valley and the London suburbs; and the quiet river valleys which weave between and through the other landscapes. Surrey is rich in strong and unexpected contrasts.

Much of historic Surrey's distinctive and varying character results from the marked grain of its geology. Successive bands of sedimentary rocks run across the county, each with its own varying ability to resist erosion. As the county lies on the north side of the wealden uplift or anticlyne, the strata generally slope downwards to the north and the ranges of hills present steep scarp faces to the south. The county is drained by a series of rivers which run northwards to the Thames, except, that is, for where the vagaries of river capture have allowed the Arun to extend northwards and to drain part of the Surrey Weald directly into the English Channel. Of the northward-flowing rivers, the Wey and Mole have cut deep gaps through the central chalk downland.

The earliest hint of man's activity is provided by flint handaxes and flake tools made between 350,000 and 10,000 years ago during the Old Stone (palaeolithic) Age. Most of these come from the terraces of the Thames and Wey laid down during the Ice Age. Because of the enormous climatic and landscape changes which have occurred since the start of that long period, almost all of the artefacts found have been carried far from their original point of deposition and man cannot be thought of as influencing the landscape at that time.

After the last glaciation, climatic conditions slowly improved and the permafrost gradually thawed out. Lichens, grasses and sedges colonized the landscape, then came birch and aspen scrub followed by pine and hazel and, finally, mixed deciduous forest in which oak, elm, alder and small-leaved lime were the dominant trees. Eventually, small communities of Middle Stone Age (mesolithic) man moved into this forest, eking out an existence by collecting berries, nuts and roots; fishing in the rivers and streams; and trapping and hunting animals. From the distribution of scatters of characteristic implements of the period, it is evident that man ranged widely over the greensand hills, along the dip-slope of the North Downs, and close to the Thames and its tributaries.

Study of deposits of fossil pollen has shown a marked and widespread decline in the elm a little under 5000 years ago. For many years this has been thought to have been caused by the activities of neolithic (New Stone Age) farmers but the possibility has recently been raised that an early outbreak of Dutch elm disease was really to blame. Nevertheless, man did begin to effect profound changes upon his environment from this time onwards.

Between 4000 and 2000 BC, the woodland was being cleared while grazing and cultivation was extending over cleared ground and more permanent settlements were being established. Some of the archaeological sites that can be recognized from the neolithic period in the Thames valley on the edge of Surrey were substantial works and imply a sizeable and stable population with a considerable capacity for organization. On the chalk downs, contemporary flint implements are found widely; a long barrow was once to be seen near Farnham and flint mines may have existed at Horsley and Woldingham.

A new type of burial practice—by single inhumation beneath a round barrow—signalled the arrival of people using bronze tools and weaponry. There are still barrows to be seen on the Greensand, the Chalk and even on the Bagshot Sands, but aerial photography has shown that many more probably existed on the valley gravels where they have been levelled by later cultivation or destroyed by gravel extraction. Little is known of the contemporary settlements but, by the Late Bronze Age, some enclosed hilltop sites, such as that now covered by Queen Mary's Hospital for Children at Carshalton, have been recognized as well as farmsteads like that excavated at Weston Wood, Albury. A more sizeable settlement is known to have existed on the county boundary at Runnymede in an ideal position to control or exploit river-borne trade. Agriculture was intensified, especially on the gravel terraces of the Thames.

Iron implements begin to appear in the archaeological record around 800 BC. The rising population caused increasing competition for land and the emergence of a more warlike society, reflected in the earthen-ramparted forts crowning St George's Hill in the Thames Valley; Cardinal's Cap on the downs south of Caterham; at Hascombe, Holmbury and Anstiebury on the Greensand; and at Dry Hill in the extreme south-east of the county. Small univallate enclosures, such as Caesar's Camp, Wimbledon, were superseded by the larger and more formidable multi-vallate hillforts listed.

It is uncertain whether any of the Surrey hillforts were occupied on a long-term basis as was the case of hillforts in other parts of England. The forts on the Greensand do not seem to have been completed and it is possible that they were built in the face of a military threat that materialized all too quickly.

Traces of the field systems of the time are still to be found at

George Philip & Son Limited

27A Floral Street London WC2E 9DP
Tel: 01-836 7863 or 01-836 1915 Telex: 21667
Publishers and Cartographers – Established 1834

Incorporating: Georama, Osprey Publishing and Stanford Maritime

10.5.88.

Msauge

el Cathy Lowne
Editorial Assistant

With Compliments

Farthing Down, Box Hill and Mickleham Downs and were formerly visible on Fetcham and Leatherhead Downs. An unenclosed farming settlement with storage pits has been excavated at Hawk's Hill, near Fetcham. Aerial photography and excavation have shown that the gravels of the Thames and its tributaries continued to be intensively farmed at this time. Aerial photography has also shown one of the characteristic 'banjo' enclosures near Tattenham Corner—and another appears from an eighteenth-century account to have existed south of Effingham. This type of enclosure is so called from its long entrance droveway and roughly circular shape and is thought to have been associated with ranching.

The Roman occupation of south-east England was accomplished in AD 43 without effective opposition. Engineered roads were cut through the landscape and linked with a network of minor roads inherited from the later prehistoric centuries. Surrey became part of the hinterland of the new Roman city of *Londinium* and no town grew up in Romano-British times in what was later to become the county. A large undefended village at Ewell may have acted as a market centre and there may have been staging posts on Stane Street—the road from London to Chichester—at Merton and near Dorking. A suburb of London was born at the south end of the bridge over the Thames and, opposite the north-west corner of the county, the thriving small town of Pontes, now Staines, was established on the road to Silchester.

In many parts of the countryside, farmsteads and small villages continued a way of life little affected by Romanization but along the gault vale there was a significant series of villas whose occupants aspired to a more comfortable way of life. Further south, a large villa near Ewhurst flourished from the first century through to the fourth.

Mixed farming was intensified and clay deposits in the county were exploited for tile-making and potting. There were religious sites of importance at Farley Heath and Wanborough and there was a small temple near Titsey on the other side of the county.

There are many unanswered questions about the end of the Roman occupation but it is from this period that the county of Surrey originates. Surrey can be said to have no identity before the *Adventus Saxoni* that followed the departure of the legions in AD 407. That part of the county now largely covered by London's sprawl was the cradle of Surrey.

The early versions of the name—*Suthergeona* in Bede; *Sothereye* in Robert of Gloucester; *Suthrige* or *Suthrege* in the *Anglo-Saxon Chronicle*—point to a meaning of the 'southern district'. This suggests that Surrey was once part of a small kingdom, probably a short-lived kingdom of the 'Middle Saxons', divided into two regions by the Thames. Place-names and excavated burial grounds show the settlement of the pagan English beginning in the fifth century with colonization throughout the sixth.

Pagan burials at Croydon and Mitcham dated to the first decades of the fifth century suggest the recruitment of Anglo-Saxon mercenaries by local communities to provide protection in a time of increasing uncertainty and instability. Over the next few decades, more and more Anglo-Saxon peoples settled in north-east Surrey. Before long they had wrested political supremacy from the lingering sub-Roman authorities.

The whole of Surrey north of the downs must have been settled, however thinly in parts, before the conversion of its people to Christianity. The river valleys and the the distribution of favourable soils determined the early settlement pattern. Cemeteries, possibly dating from a pagan resurgence in the mid-seventh century under the Mercian king, Penda, have been excavated on the downs at Coulsdon and Banstead. Other less vigorously pagan cemeteries have been found on the downs at Tattenham Corner, Leatherhead and Guildford. Settlement had probably reached the gault vale at Godstone, Reigate and Dorking by the end of the century, if not earlier. Pagan place-names in south-west Surrey and at Thunderfield, near Horley, may represent settlements where paganism lingered on the fringe of a county nominally Christian but still unconvinced of the ineffectiveness of the old gods.

The pagan English inherited cleared land and a road system from their Romano-British predecessors. The roads were probably only of limited use to the incomers but parts of Stane Street and the London–Portslade road seem to have remained in use and part of the London–Lewes road north of the downs was to become the boundary between Surrey and Kent.

To the south, east and west, Surrey was bordered by the growing kingdoms of Sussex, Kent and Wessex. Between Surrey and Sussex stretched the Weald, a natural barrier of a fairly formidable kind, but Surrey seems to have been fought over more than once during disputes between Wessex and Kent. It is likely that the West Saxon victory of 568, when Ceawlin and Cutha fought with Ethelbert 'and drove him into Kent', was followed by a period of West Saxon rule in Surrey. However, a charter granting lands to Chertsey Abbey in around 675 seems to indicate that Surrey then had its own *sub-regulus*, Frithwald, had been under the supremacy of Egbert I of Kent (664–73) when the abbey was founded and was, at the time of the charter, under the supremacy of Wulfhere of Mercia who had crushingly defeated the West Saxons shortly before. By 688, Caedwalla, King of Wessex, was undoubtedly master of west Surrey but changes of mastery continued into the eighth century. In the ninth century Surrey became permanently attached to the enlarged West Saxon kingdom by King Egbert.

Such political changes may have had little effect on the way of life of the peasantry. Early agricultural methods seem to have included transhumance (summer pasturage) using common pasturing grounds on the downs and even in the Weald. The wealden pastures were used by settlements to the north—in east Surrey, well to the north after the Kentish fashion. By the time of the first charters in the tenth and eleventh centuries, the woodland around the communal lands in the Weald was breaking up into separately held pig farms and becoming permanently, if sparsely, occupied.

In 851 or 852, the storm of Danish invasion burst upon south-east England. After wintering in Thanet, the Danes burnt Canterbury, passed up the Thames and sacked London. Only Winchester and her kings stood between the Danes and rule of southern England. But the West Saxons under Alfred defeated the Danes in a battle possibly fought on Surrey soil, near Ockley.

As the Danish invasions became more frequent they came near to destroying the independence of Wessex. But Alfred the Great and Edward the Elder regained the initiative and established a strategic network of regional defence centres known as *burhs*. These were to become the basis of a revival of the town life that had failed after the end of the Roman occupation.

Surrey contributed to the grand Wessex design for defence against the Danes and fortified *burhs* were established at Eashing and Southwark. That at Eashing was soon to be replaced by a market settlement at Guildford, carved out of a corner of the ancient royal estate of Stoke. Southwark, the bridgehead south of London, shared in the fortunes of the city. It was probably at this time that London's influence over Surrey began to be felt more generally, an influence that was to grow until today nearly half the ancient county can be thought of as part of London itself or to be largely suburban in character.

By the time of Alfred, the settlement pattern that was to prevail until comparatively modern times had probably become firmly established. Prosperous (although not necessarily nucleated) villages existed in the Thames valley and along the dip-slope spring line of the North Downs. The villages on the spring line extended their influence and resource base southwards on the Chalk and northwards on to the London Clay. Smaller settlements had grown up at favourable places on the chalk downs themselves. To the south, in the gault vale, the limited fertile soils were being fully exploited by a long line of closely spaced settlements that extended *their* influence and resource base to the top of the downs in one direction and across the sandy woodlands of the greensand hills onto the clay of the Weald in the other. Some parts of Surrey were to take up something resembling the Midland style of open-field strip cultivation by the later Middle Ages but the characteristic pattern of ridge and furrow only survives in the county in a few, barely discernible patches.

After the Norman conquest, the late Saxon towns and larger villages were thought to represent a threat to King William and he soon took steps to ensure his control of them, building strong castles at strategic places like Guildford and encouraging his barons to follow his example. The royal castle at Guildford, like a number of others up and down the country, started life as a motte-and-bailey but the timber palisades and buildings were soon to be replaced in stone. Guildford castle was accompanied by a park and other Norman castles and manor houses also had their own parks, for the Normans were great hunters and fond of the chase.

Most medieval parks were broken up for farmland in the Tudor period but, in some cases, such as that of the former park at Lagham in south Godstone, the distinctive curved outline of their boundaries can still be traced among the modern fields.

The parks served specifically as enclosures for deer. They were wild areas of wood and pasture, surrounded by a paling fence with an internal ditch to prevent the deer escaping. The king's own park at Guildford was the most important of these in Surrey and leaves a reminder in the name of Stag Hill on which the cathedral now stands.

Important to the Norman kings was the existence of royal forests, areas in which the king's hunt had priority over other uses of the land. Partly spilling into Surrey, and at one time threatening to absorb the whole county, was Windsor Forest. While the king's forests were in no sense continuous areas of unbroken woodland, they did include many woods to provide cover for the deer and within the forest there were numerous parks.

During the Middle Ages, Surrey's settlement pattern was consolidated but there were few, if any, dramatic changes. Churches were rebuilt, altered and enlarged. Trade developed and travel became easier. New market boroughs were founded at Haslemere, Reigate and Bletchingley—the last two in place of earlier rural communities on nearby sites. None of these—and few of the other places in Surrey that had or developed market rights at this time—achieved urban status. Only Southwark, Guildford, Kingston and, to a lesser extent, Farnham could really be called towns in medieval Surrey. The proximity of London appears to have inhibited the growth of urban centres.

The growth of market towns in the two centuries and a half after the Norman conquest was matched by the development of industries, many of them in the countryside. New industries emerged, old ones developed and trades and occupations became increasingly specialized.

The two centuries from 1300 were characterized by decline and decay with only slow and uneven recovery. Decline started before the arrival of the Black Death but the economic recession was not uniform across the kingdom. Certain areas seem to have been favoured and may have avoided the general fall in population and prosperity. Surrey, along with other counties close to London, appears to have been such an area as consideration of village desertion tends to show.

Desertions do not seem to be evidenced everywhere and convincing signs of deserted medieval villages are singularly infrequent in the vicinity of London. This may be, in part at least, because later emparkment and landscaping or later rebuilding and reoccupation has covered erstwhile traces of abandoned settlements. But on the whole it seems to be because desertion was rare.

Surrey provides only a handful of genuine desertions and only a few more examples where the evidence is ambiguous. Many examples that have been cited were actually probably never deserted and others were never villages.

The phenomenon of desertion is not totally absent, however. Classic 'sheep farming' depopulations have been identified on the Chalk south of Croydon at Woodcote and Watendone. At Beddington, the twin villages of Beddington and Bandon seem to have been reduced to one by late medieval emparkment. At Waddon it is uncertain whether a deserted settlement actually met the modest minimum requirements to justify the term 'village'.

By the fifteenth century, wealthy London merchants had become interested in Surrey real estate and came to retire as landowners. Monumental brasses depicting them in civilian dress are a distinctive feature of Surrey churches—for example, at Bletchingly, Farleigh and Mickleham. Sixteenth-century civilians also commemorated by Surrey brasses include a number of officials of the royal households of Sheen, Nonsuch, Oatlands and Hampton Court; public officers like sheriffs and keepers of royal parks; and a numerous group of city businessmen. Engraved with men in close-fitting medieval tunics or in the ruffs and doublets fashionable in the sixteenth century, these brasses are proof of the steadily increasing place in Surrey life of residents connected with the political, legal and commercial life of the nation.

Henry Tudor rebuilt the old royal manor of Sheen with magnificence and gave it the name of Richmond from the earldom he had held before Bosworth. The name gradually supplanted that of Sheen for the whole town which grew up around the palace. It was one of the last truly medieval palaces in a style which only gave way gradually to new architectural ideas of classical inspiration.

One of the earliest signs in England of the influence of the Renaissance on architecture was at Sutton Place, near Woking, built *c*1523–5 by Sir Richard Weston, a member of Henry VIII's court. The design appears to have been influenced by the chateaux Weston had visited on his travels on the king's business in the country of the Loire. Sutton Place was built of brick and terracotta around a quadrangular space fronted by an arched gateway flanked by lofty hexagonal towers. The house survives but not the arched gateway and flanking towers.

The king himself was an enthusiastic builder and built Nonsuch and Oatlands Palaces in Surrey. At one time, Richmond was in danger of being eclipsed by Nonsuch Palace as *the* royal residence in the county.

When Henry VIII came to build Nonsuch, he employed artists from northern Europe and Italy and heaped their products around a vast, near-symmetrical double courtyard. The outside was pargetted and slate-hung in a scheme that was as much grotesque as decorative. The ordinary architectural style of Surrey at the time, however, had nothing to do with the excesses of Nonsuch ore even with the innovations of Sutton Place, but carried on a simplified late Gothic style with gables and mullion-and-transome windows right into Elizabethan and Jacobean times.

By 1539 the Dissolution had occurred and the despotism of Church and State was fully established. The earlier changes wrought by the first two Tudor kings had probably had little impact in most villages and life may have remained unaltered. But the Dissolution brought about the redistribution of vast numbers of estates, the largest redistribution since the time of William the Conquerer, and some men rapidly acquired immense wealth through the seizure of the former monastic lands.

As the monastic wealth was diverted from the Church it was poured into more elaborate domestic buildings such as Loseley and the now lost Wimbledon House, and into benefactions such as schools and almshouses. From the time of the Tudors, there was a growing tendency for the rich city merchants, lawyers and courtiers to migrate to the less crowded and more healthy countryside south of the Thames. In the nineteenth century, this movement was to increase to such an extent that whole districts became covered by country houses with large gardens.

Before the enclosures and the Industrial Revolution stamped out local crafts and industry, Surrey was an important manufacturing county. By the sixteenth and seventeenth centuries the Wey, Tillingbourne, Mole and Wandle rivers had been harnessed to provide motive power to work mills making iron, brass, cloth, paper and gunpowder. Some of the mills survived until the late nineteenth century as flour or grist mills and many broken dams and dried or disused mill and hammer ponds can be found in the landscape.

From the seventeenth century, the face of Surrey has also been repeatedly reshaped by successive generations striving to achieve ideal forms of landscape. Early eighteenth-century travellers had imputed to the landscape many of the virtues conventionally ascribed to a garden. The soft, garden-like quality of the Surrey scene away from heaths and the higher parts of the bare downs conformed to this conventionally accepted notion of the beautiful and, consequently, Surrey came to be esteemed as a district where garden-like scenery could be created cheaply and perfectly.

To John Evelyn, polymath diarist of Wotton and founder member of the Royal Society, Surrey was 'the county of my Birth and my Delight'. He shared the growing interest in agriculture which was the mark of the English gentleman of his day and was interested in botany, becoming more and more absorbed in trees. His favourite species were those characteristic of Surrey—the oak, ash, elm and beech as well as its native evergreens: the holly, yew, privet and box. In addition he involved himself in the acclimatization of fir and pine in his own part of Surrey.

Most of the pinewoods that today are seen as an enrichment of the Surrey landscape originate in planting no earlier than the late eighteenth century but the thick pinewoods running from Wotton to the summit of Leith Hill began in part in Evelyn's planting of a century before. The landscaping by the Evelyn brothers which made Wotton the most famous garden in the mid seventeenth century is recorded by John Evelyn in his *Diary* and in his own etchings. Another outstanding garden by Evelyn on Italian lines was at Albury Park.

In the seventeenth century, mansions such as Moor Park and Ham House were surrounded by formal gardens set within the deer parks, and landscape parks themselves increasingly came to be regarded as an important part of the setting of the great house. Up to the early eighteenth century formal designs with long, straight avenues and canals were fashionable. In the 1730s, however, there was a significant break from the formal tradition with the work of Southcote at Woburn, near Chertsey, James Hamilton at Painshill and William Kent at Claremont and Esher. A little later, the new Clandon House (built in the 1730s) was surrounded by a park laid out by Capability Brown.

Lancelot 'Capability' Brown introduced the planting of circular clumps and screens of beech trees. Park design was regarded as so important that, on occasion, entire villages (such as Titsey and Albury) would be swept away in order to preserve the landscape. Today, much of the delicate balance between pleasure and utility created at such cost has been abandoned but something survives of the landscape created by George Lock at Norbury under the influence of Capability Brown.

Surrey's wilder hilly and heathy tracts were not aesthetically appreciated until the impulse of the Romantic and Picturesque movement towards the end of the eighteenth century—and not always then. With the growing predilection for such 'wild' places, however, these parts of the county were colonized in the latter part of the nineteenth century by people intent on playing the role of country gentry.

The reconciliation between man and land in Surrey as worked out over the experience of many centuries produced, by the late eighteenth century, an exceptionally variegated scenery that was exerting a strong fascination upon artists, composers, men of letters and naturalists. The rapid and complete changes of scenery inspired the artist J.M.W. Turner (1775–1851) during his many journeys across Surrey to Petworth House, the home of his patron, Lord Egremont. Numerous pencil sketches preserved in many notebooks record his visual pleasure at glimpses of the varied and richly wooded Surrey landscape where 'at every turn some fresh picture opened upon us'.

William Cobbett (1762–1835), on the other hand, was less than captivated by the wilder aspects of scenery. His ability to infer the influence exerted by the sub-soil on surface cultivation has probably never been equalled and he expressed the scenic variety of Surrey in agricultural terms:

> *The county of Surrey presents to the eye of the traveller a*
> *greater contrast than any other county in England. It has*
> *some of the very best and some of the worst lands, not only*
> *in England, but in the world.*

Cobbett railed against the evil uses to which the water power of the Tillingbourne was being put but, in a rare record of aesthetic satisfaction, he also penned a word picture of the diverse country of the Wey valley between Godalming and Guildford:

> *Here are hill and dell in endless variety. Here are Chalk*
> *and sand, vieing with each other in making beautiful scenes.*
> *Here are woods and downs. Here is something of everything*
> *but fat marshes and those skeleton-making agues.*

The climate of agricultural improvements, landscape development and industrial expansion demanded improvements in the transport system. Since the sixteenth century each parish had been responsible for the upkeep of roads within its bounds but they were usually poorly maintained. A new series of Turnpike Acts gave local trusts the power to levy a toll upon road users in order to pay for their repair and, by the beginning of Victoria's reign, a network of improved turnpike roads had spread all over the county. Stage-coach services were able to take full advantage of the improved road surfaces and coaching inns appeared on many of the main roads. Most of these have now disappeared from the county along with most of the once characteristic bow-fronted toll houses that have been sacrificed to road-widening.

The River Thames had been navigable throughout the Middle Ages. The Thames Commissioners established in 1770 continued works of improvement making new navigation cuts at Walton and Chertsey. Surrey, however, saw a much earlier and remarkable feat of river control. Regulating the flow of rivers and making them navigable by sluices and locks seems to have been common in Lombardy and in the Netherlands before the seventeenth century and was introduced into France under Henri IV. Pound locks were installed on the Thames near Oxford before 1638 and Sir Richard Weston of Sutton Place had seen the use of locks in the Low Countries and introduced them into Surrey. In 1651 he obtained an Act of Parliament for making the Wey navigable by means of locks between Guildford and its junction with the Thames. Work started in 1653, but took many years to see fruition. There were quarrels among the shareholders and difficulties with others and it was not until another Act had been obtained in 1671 that the matter was settled.

Oak for shipbuilding could now be brought this way from the Weald to the Thames. The importance of the canal can be gauged by seventeenth-century evidence that in some weeks 500 or 600 quarters of corn or meal were carried. In the nineteenth century paper and gunpowder from the mills on the Tillingbourne at Chilworth were also carried downstream on the canal.

A century ago sailing barges were common on the Thames but today only a handful survive and are cherished by aficionados, although they are seldom seen as far upstream as Richmond. In this photograph are one traditional Thames sailing barge and two lighter barges, just upstream of Richmond railway bridge. On the other hand rowing skiffs are now rare on the Thames as far downstream as this foreshore and usually lack the elegance of their Victorian and Edwardian predecessors.

After the great impetus to canal-making had been given by the Duke of Bridgewater and Brindley, the engineer, the Wey navigation was extended further upstream to Godalming by an Act of Parliament of 1760. In 1796 the Basingstoke Canal was completed, coming from north Hampshire into the Wey navigation near Byfleet. Military camps at Aldershot ensured that this branch of the canal remained open well into the twentieth century. The Wey navigation remains in use for pleasure craft and is now owned by the National Trust. The Surrey Canal was made in accordance with an Act of 1801, from a dock at Rotherhithe to Camberwell, across the levels without a lock. It was intended originally to be carried on to the Thames again at Vauxhall. The Croydon Canal was projected at the time and ran from Croydon through part of Surrey and Kent to join the Surrey Canal at Deptford.

The system of water carriage connected with the Wey was completed by another canal that left the river halfway between Guildford and Godalming and led to the Arun above Pulborough. The Act for its construction was obtained in 1813 and the canal was opened shortly afterwards. The end of the Napoleonic wars, however, meant that the anticipated transfer of trade from coasters to the canal never took place and the canal was a financial failure.

The Wey and Arun Canal soon became a thing of the past. By 1873 it was barely passable for a small boat and by the end of the century it had in many places been filled up and abandoned. But the coming of the railways led to the neglect and failure of more than the Wey and Arun Canal. The Croydon Canal had been purchased in 1836 by the Croydon Railway Company and became partly used by the line of the London, Brighton and South Coast and South-Eastern Railways.

Surrey can boast not only of one of the first canalized rivers but also of the first public railway. This was the horse-drawn plateway set up from Wandsworth to Croydon under an Act of 1802 and later extended to Merstham. Its principal object was to aid the carriage of lime and building materials from Croydon to the Thames and the many factories of various kinds which stood near it also used the railway. A project to connect the Wey and Arun Canal to the railway terminus at Merstham came to nothing, which is hardly surprising, and, in fact, the extension south from Croydon to Merstham was not successful.

The earliest railway worked by locomotive engines in the London neighbourhood also started in Surrey. On 26 December 1838, the London and Greenwich line was opened with great ceremony: the terminus at the London end was where London Bridge Station now stands. The Croydon Railway followed in 1839, the Brighton line and the South-Western line to Southampton were opened in 1840, and the Dover Railway was completed from Redhill to Dover in 1842.

The coming of first the turnpikes and then the railways brought suburban London to the north-eastern part of the county followed by the expansion of Croydon, Guildford and Horley and the creation of 'railway towns' at New Woking, Redhill and Surbiton. The expansion of London covered thousands of acres of farmland, commonland and park with small houses. Nevertheless, at the close of the nineteenth century Surrey was still considered to be 'the most delightful rural suburb of London' (by H.E. Maldon in his *History of Surrey*) but the same writer noted that the county was 'increasingly studded with country houses which belong to those who are desirous of combining a dwelling in beautiful country with ready access to London'. He also warned that 'the north-eastern parts of it are daily encroached upon by the growing cancer of brickwork which, settling upon the beauties of woods and downs, gradually devours them with a monotonous hideousness of streets'.

Between the two World Wars, motor cars and electric trains brought a further exodus out of London into Surrey. By the late 1920s, the streets of many Surrey towns were congested by motor traffic and the West Surrey Regional Town Planning Authority recommended the building of bypasses. The construction of the Guildford and Godalming bypass was completed in 1934 under a government scheme of public works to relieve unemployment in the county. Meanwhile the destructive ugliness of the speculative builder was threatening some of the finest scenery in the county. This process was to continue, checked only by philanthropy and the National Trust, until the Green Belt policies of 1945 on called a halt. Even now the containment of the wen is far from complete and the Green Belt itself is threatened as never before. The engineers and politicians who designed London's orbital motorway found that it provided a ready corridor, and now developers, ever eager for the more profitable 'green field' sites close to 'good communications', fight a continuing war of attrition.

Surrey beyond the suburbs is today very much a county for recreation and of passage. Between Greater London and the greensand scarp, where the landscape is not actually urban or suburban, it is difficult to shake off the feeling of being in a huge park. Through this semi-parkland traffic hurries, or tries to hurry, along the motorways and trunk roads to Gatwick, to the south coast or westwards towards Portsmouth or Basingstoke. With the opening of the orbital motorway, traffic from the Kent ports to the Midlands now drives across the county, while seemingly never-ending demands for housing constitutes an unrelenting pressure on what is left of Surrey's scenic and once rural landscape.

Map Section

The Dutch House at Kew in about 1890.

KEY TO ONE INCH MAPS

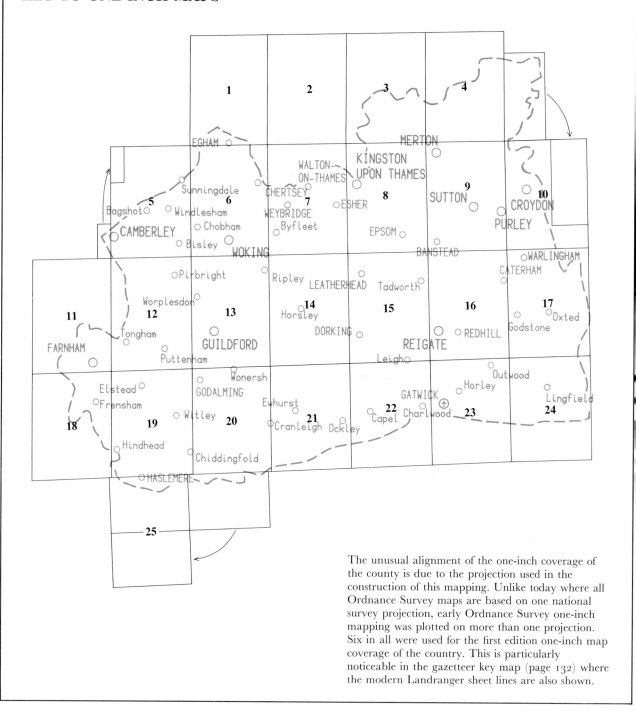

The unusual alignment of the one-inch coverage of the county is due to the projection used in the construction of this mapping. Unlike today where all Ordnance Survey maps are based on one national survey projection, early Ordnance Survey one-inch mapping was plotted on more than one projection. Six in all were used for the first edition one-inch map coverage of the country. This is particularly noticeable in the gazetteer key map (page 132) where the modern Landranger sheet lines are also shown.

Map 1

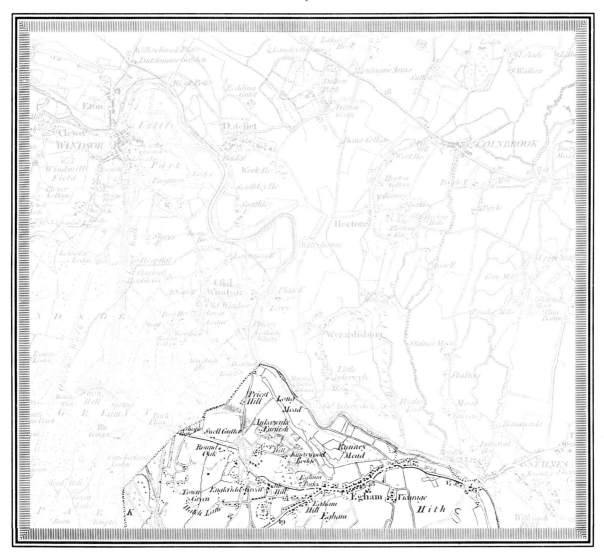

Map 1 Surrey has seen few major events in English history but, just within the county boundary at its north-western extremity near Egham, *Magna Carta* was signed in 1215. A rather characterless but popular public open space by the Thames is now preserved to commemorate the event.

On the north bank of the Thames, Surrey has acquired a sector of Middlesex, the district of Spelthorne, transferred in 1975. This includes Staines, a small market town in 1822 but a settlement of Roman origin.

Map 2

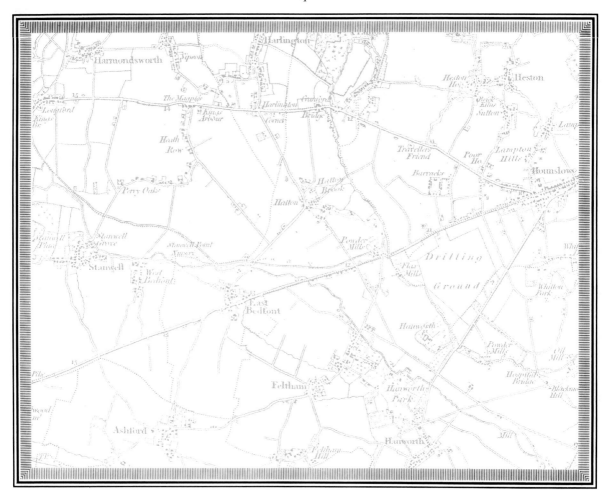

Map 2 (above) Stanwell, with its attractive green, and Ashford are historically part of Middlesex. The villages of Sunbury, Shepperton and Laleham (see Map 7) have much more to offer.

---◇◇◇---

Map 3 (opposite) Richmond takes its name from the palace built here by Henry Tudor, who was formerly the Duke of Richmond. The park of more than 800ha (2000 acres) was established by Charles I in 1637 in an act of arrogance that was one of many which fuelled the growing engine of revolution.

The Georgians saw Richmond as a country retreat and it did not experience the urban development of Bath or Cheltenham. Richmond's riverside scenery and accessibility, however, made it an attractive resort and society flocked there in the wake of the enthusiastic patronage of the Hanoverian royalty. In the map of 1822 (with the mid-century railways added) Richmond is seen much as the eighteenth century had left it.

Horace Walpole's correspondence tells us much about the eighteenth-century use of Richmond by the fashionable of London, who left their town houses in Westminster to come here for summer weekends. The eldest son of George I resided at Richmond Lodge, a Palladian house formerly standing in the grounds of the Old Deer Park near the

Map 3

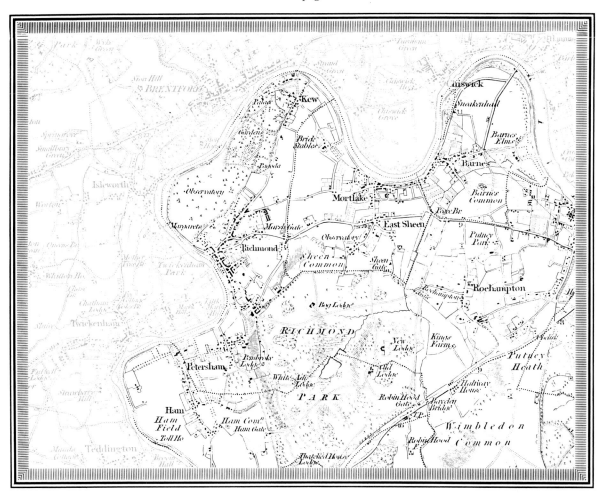

observatory. On his accession as George II, White Lodge was built for him in Richmond Park. His son, Frederick, Prince of Wales, remodelled the White House at Kew, now demolished. George III lived there and his children were provided with houses on or near Kew Green.

Richmond remained a popular upper-class residential area throughout the nineteenth century although there was some slight shift down the social scale.

The nineteenth century saw the gradual spread of housing over north-east Surrey—reaching as far as the villas of Putney Hill and Richmond. Lords of the manor attempted to cash in on the boom in building land and to enclose commons for housing. They were resisted by the Commons Preservation Society and its solicitor, Sir Robert Hunter, later to be a founder of the National Trust. One of the most notable victories for the movement was the defence of Wimbledon Common, threatened by the ancestor of the present Princess of Wales. At the end of the struggle, the then Earl Spencer obtained a compensating perpetual annuity of £1200 per year in return for not enclosing the common. Ironically, in view of the scandal that surrounded its creation, Richmond Park, as crown land, was free from such pressures.

Map 4

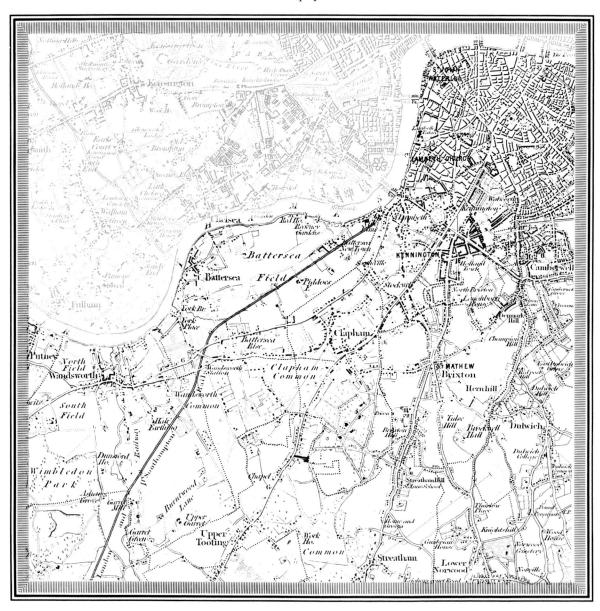

Map 4 At the turn of the eighteenth and nineteenth centuries, the lower Wandle valley was an important industrial area. In 1802, an Act of Parliament authorized the construction of a railway from Croydon to Wandsworth for the use of the public. This was the Surrey Iron Railway, the first public railway in England (see also map on page 56). It was built for the carriage by horse-drawn trucks of goods and minerals, mainly lime and building materials. As the industries of the Wandle Valley had been greatly stimulated by the Industrial Revolution, several factories of various kinds stood near the railway and made use of it. Its success led to the construction of an ill-judged extension from Croydon to Merstham.

By the beginning of the nineteenth century, the villas of Camberwell, Streatham, Tooting

By the 1880s the poverty and squalor of the Surrey waterside were notorious. *In* Oliver Twist, *Dickens has provided a graphic picture of the squalor of Bermondsey around Jacob's Island, while Richard Jeffrey's* Red Roofs of London *gives a glimpse of the houses of the same parish as viewed from the trains rattling over the arches of the line between New Cross and London Bridge. The trains passed on a level with garrets containing 'women and children with scarce room to move, the bed and dining table in the same apartment'. Conditions in Lambeth were hardly different.*

The riverfront upstream of Lambeth Palace was largely industrial in the nineteenth century and its appearance was greatly changed by the construction of the Albert Embankment from Vauxhaul to Westminster Bridge (below). The gradual erection of a cliff of multi-storey offices since the Second World War has changed its appearance again (right).

Map 4 cont.

and Clapham, however unlikely it may seem now, were the homes of the new merchant class: dignified, correct, church-going, and utterly conformist. Further out were the landed gentry and the very rich. The parish church at Clapham had been totally rebuilt in 1775 and was later associated with the Clapham Sect who were instrumental in bringing about the abolition of slavery in the early years of the nineteenth century.

Growing demand for land by speculative builders in Surrey pushed up land prices and the land was divided into house lots and sold, subdivided and sold again. 'In the hands of the builders' was a familiar sign in the countryside close to London—and further out. The commons of Clapham, Wandsworth, Barnes, Tooting and Mitcham were slashed across by the railways of the 1840s and '50s and were only saved from total destruction after a great struggle.

Charles Booth's Life and Labour of the People of London *gives the first accurate and vivid description of social life in the streets converging on the Elephant and Castle, the hub of south London in the nineteenth century. His elaborately annotated maps (which have been reproduced by the London Topographical Society) show the wider high roads coloured bright red to signify the better-off middle-class houses and small shops. These roads were crammed with new clanging trams, horse-drawn omnibuses and cabs, while poorer streets ran off them. Typical of these crowded alleys may have been Black Alley in Kentish Street, Newington, comprising fourteen tiny tenements behind the Black Bear Inn.*

Many of the buildings at 'The Elephant' were rebuilt before the Second World War but severe bomb damage and the need to redesign the busiest traffic junction in south London have meant that very little survives now from the Victorian period.

The early photograph shows an unusual view of a London Tramways car being pulled by three mules.

Experiments were made with mules in the 1890s but were not generally successful. The car has been converted from 'knifeboard' to 'garden seat' layout on the upper deck (John R. Day, London's Trams and Trolleybuses, *1977).*

Map 5 (overleaf) The most striking feature in the landscape of north-west Surrey is the great expanse of heath and coniferous woodland. Sandy beds of the Bagshot and Bracklesham series, with their occasional layers of gravels, are responsible. Large areas of Bagshot Heath are ill-drained, especially where an iron pan has formed just below the surface preventing the water from draining away. In such situations, reed and sedge prevail, with patches of cotton-grass in places.

Traversed by the road from the West Country to London, Bagshot Heath was one of the most notorious neighbourhoods for mounted highwaymen around London at the turn of the eighteenth century. This was no new development for, according to Aubrey a century earlier, Egham parish had paid more on account of robberies committed in it, chiefly on the same road, than had any other parish in England.

Map 5

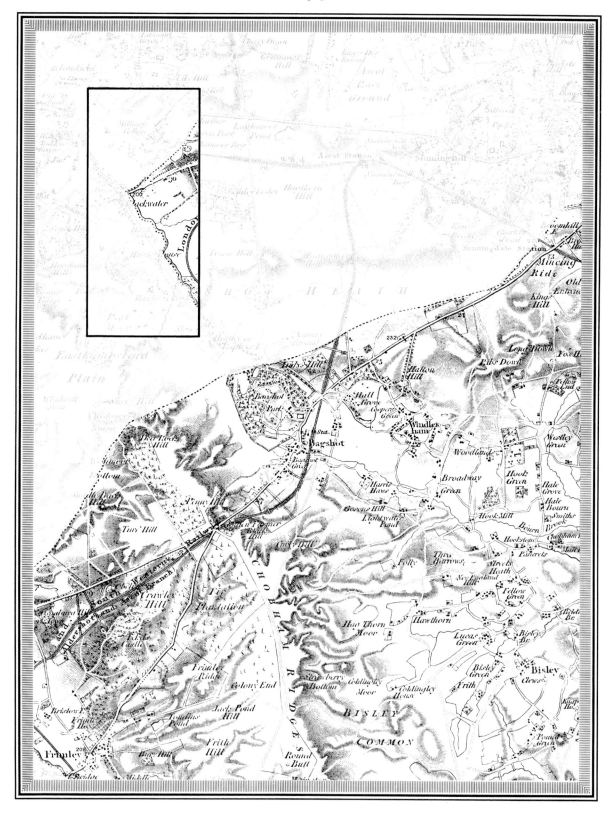

A shooting match at Bisley in 1910, between members of the Army, Navy and public.

(Overleaf) The present bridge at Chertsey was built between 1780 and 1785 by James Paine, designer of Richmond Bridge, who lived at Chertsey. It replaced a ramshackle wooden affair with origins in the fifteenth century. The parapets and balustrade of the eighteenth-century bridge have been altered and partly replaced, and other major repairs were carried out in 1820, 1892–3 and 1913.

23592 *Chaudeau Bridge & Hotel*

Map 6

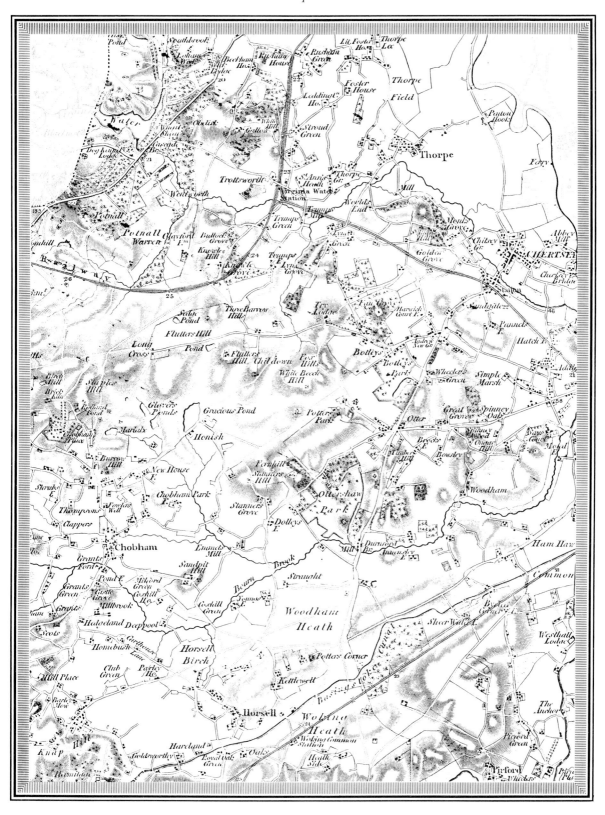

Map 6 and modern map 6 (pages 40 and 41) As with many English counties, Surrey had medieval traits that lasted into the nineteenth century. Egham, for example, still had 120ha (300 acres) of open fields in 1809, in addition to 100ha (250 acres) at Runnymede, surviving from the medieval way of farming. Similar surviving areas were to be found in other Thames-side parishes—Thorpe had 140ha (350 acres) and Chertsey 100 (250). At Egham, rent for open field land was from 20s to 25s an acre, which was above the average rent for enclosures elsewhere in the country, so the quality of the open field land must have been high.

Later the gravel flood plain of the Thames attracted market gardeners, but today motorways, housing and active and deserted gravel pits occupy most of the area. Abandoned and flooded gravel pits provide many of the marinas in the neighbourhood and form the centre of Thorpe Park.

This corner of Surrey presents a microcosm of the history of transport in England with turnpike, canal, railway and motorway.

The Basingstoke Canal was completed in 1796 and, in the middle of the nineteenth century, the railways from London to Southampton and to the West Country were routed across the heathlands. There was little in the way—and the tracks run in near straight lines and smooth, gentle curves across the map. Today London's orbital motorway, the M25, cuts a noisy swathe through what is left of the countryside—at a cost of something in the order of one and one half million pounds per mile.

A romantic view of nineteenth-century gypsies. Today hardly anyone sees the 'travelling folk' in a romantic light but local authorities are statutorily bound to provide camping sites. Once itinerant farm and woodland workers, they seem to have become itinerant scrap dealers and car breakers.

The expansion of London had reached Raynes Park by the start of the First World War. In the 1920s and 1930s, the tide of speculative building rolled inexorably over Malden, Motspur Park, Worcester Park and Cheam and reached as far as Chessington, Epsom and Ewell where Bonesgate Ford is now a busy road (above and opposite). Beyond the solidly covered portion of the county, every railway station had its landscape blot of new housing alongside: sometimes more than just a blot. It was not until the imposition of Green Belt policies in the post-war years that a halt was called.

Map 7 (page 47) Surrey is a county of vanished palaces. Kennington, Oatlands and Nonsuch have gone completely. Little is left of Richmond and less of Woking although more remains of Croydon and Lambeth Palaces.

It is hard today to believe that the Palace of Oatlands was once a structure of great extent and complexity. It was built of red brick with stone quoins and dressings, gables, bays and ornamental chimney shafts, somewhat after the fashion of Hampton Court. The foundations are said to have been traced over an area of fourteen acres.

Elizabeth I often stayed at Oatlands early in her reign. So did James I in his. Later in the seventeenth century it was razed to the ground but, in 1725, the Earl of Lincoln built a new

house in its place. This in turn was enlarged and remodelled by his grandson, the Duke of Newcastle. Horace Walpole had first thought of it as 'the centre of Paradise', although later he felt it 'not half so Elysian as I used to think'. By 1858 the house had become Oatlands Park Hotel and, soon afterwards, much of the park was built over.

This corner of Surrey was of outstanding importance in the history of English landscape gardening. Vanbrugh worked at Claremont between 1709 and 1720, Bridgeman around 1726, William Kent in the 1730s and 'Capability' Brown around 1770. The grounds at Claremont were restored by the National Trust between 1975 and 1977 and the pleasure grounds laid out for the few are

45

An engraving by Robert Wallis from a watercolour by J. M. W. Turner of the King's Marine Pavilion at Virginia Water.

Map 7 cont.

now enjoyed by many. Before the publication of the first Ordnance Survey maps, Vanbrugh's house at Claremont had been replaced by a mansion built for Clive of India by 'Capability' Brown and Henry Holland. Other important landscaped grounds were laid out in the eighteenth century by Charles Hamilton at Pains Hill and by William Kent at Esher Place.

Although projected somewhat earlier, the Wey was made navigable from the Thames to Guildford, a distance of fifteen miles, between 1651 and 1653 by Sir Richard Weston of Sutton Place (see map on page 74). The work

Map 7

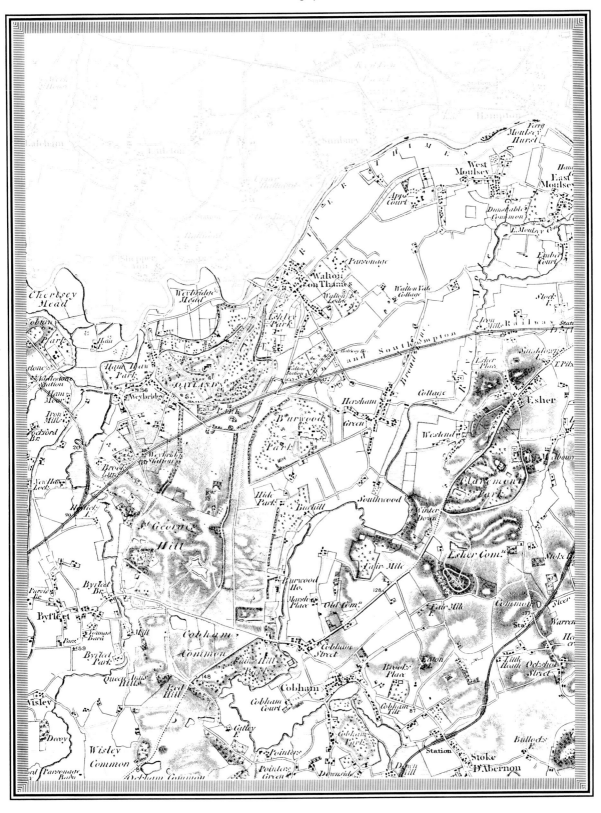

Bridge Road, Molesey, in 1910.

1664. Later, gunpowder was brought down from Chilworth and, in 1730, the Weybridge Vestry complained about the danger of its storage in the village.

Map 7 cont.
involved the construction of cuttings and locks at a cost of £15,000. It has every claim to be one of the earliest navigations of its kind in England and materials taken from the demolition of Oatlands Palace are said to have been used in the construction of the locks. Although the canal lay outside the parish of Weybridge, its confluence with the Thames brought trade to the town and watermen's cottages were built at the north end of Thames Street.

In the early years of the canal, its chief cargoes appear to have been timber, some four thousand loads coming from Guildford in

Map 8 and modern map 8 (overleaf) In the nineteenth century, two isolated Surrey towns were to be found on this portion of the map: Kingston upon Thames and Epsom. Their histories could hardly have been more different.

Kingston had been of considerable importance in the Middle Ages when it possessed the first bridge across the Thames upstream from London. Recent archaeological excavations have exposed remains of the medieval bridge and of contemporary houses and pottery kilns.

Kingston was not then the county town, a role played by Guildford. After the removal of

Map 8

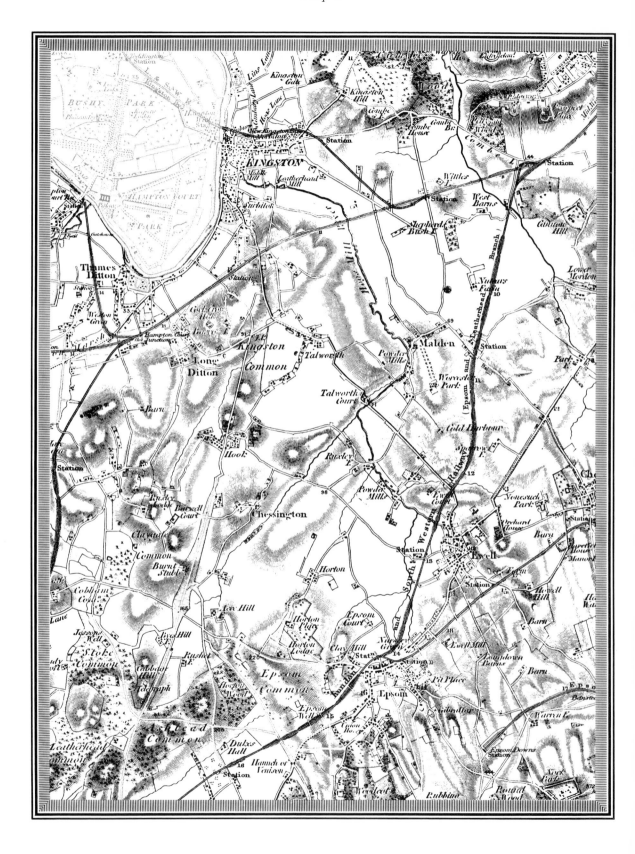

Map 8 and modern map 8 cont.

a slice of Surrey to help to form the new county of London in 1889, and in the face of the immense pull of London—by then it was the place to which Surrey people naturally went for business and for amusement—Guildford was unable to maintain itself as a real capital. Various towns claimed the right to be the seat of the county's administration, and in the event the lot fell upon Kingston. Since 1965, when Kingston itself was absorbed into the newly created and short-lived Metropolitan County of Greater London, consideration has again been given to the claims of Guildford, but financial constraints have prevented any move from Kingston.

Epsom, by contrast, had not existed as a town before the end of the seventeenth century and owed its rise to the discovery of medicinal springs. The 'taking of the waters' was a fashionable cure for those who could afford it, even before the seventeenth century, but England was not supposed to possess medicinal springs for drinking. The Bath waters were certainly widely known as medicinal for bathing and probably many places had a local reputation. But the discovery of the Epsom wells so near London, marked in their medicinal action and sufficiently nasty to command faith, was a new development for England and started our first great and fashionable watering place. A shed to cover the drinkers from the rain and a fence around the well to keep off the cattle—which, in any case, had the good sense not to drink the water—were sufficient accommodation at first. But Epsom salts became famous and, by the end of the century, Epsom had become a spa town. It reached the height of its popularity as a spa about a century later but never seems to have had any great architectural pretentions.

The contrast between the two maps can hardly be greater than it is for the area between Kingston and Epsom. In 1816, the landscape was one of small farms. Today, three-quarters or more of the land surface is covered by roads, railways, houses and their gardens and much of the open land north of Epsom has been earmarked for housing in the recently proposed changes in the county plan.

Kingston Bridge has been in existence since before 1200, and its presence no doubt helped Kingston's growth as a market town. Henry III granted the right to hold a fair here in 1256; it was to continue for eight days and included a cattle market.

Camden in his Britannica, *written in 1586, says that 'a market is held weekly at Kingston on Saturdays; it is kept on a green field and is so big [that] indeed it may pass for a fair.' This 'green field' may be the present Fairfield, since the market place could never have been big enough to warrant Camden's description (left, and see also page 52). It was, however, used as a cattle market in the nineteenth century until this became too large and successful to continue there and had to be resited.*

Epsom has greatly changed since the early photograph (above) was taken. It grew into a town following the discovery in 1618 of the properties of a local spring, but much has been lost from the 'spa' period, especially in the High Street. The last twenty years have seen wholesale changes in the western half of the High Street, but it may still be 'the widest and breeziest main street of any Surrey town', and the grotesque clock tower of 1847–8 survives (opposite).

Map 9 (overleaf) The main feature of the chalk dip slope covered by the southern half of the map is the series of dry valleys. In their characteristic development, they deeply dissect the original chalk surface. Towards the lower end of the dry valleys, close to the junction of the Chalk and the overlying Thanet Sand, occasional streams or bournes used to break out after periods of wet weather and flowed for a time on the valley floor. One of the best known was that at Croydon, near the headwaters of the River Wandle. Before the course of the bourne was covered over in 1882, its waters periodically flooded the marshy floor of the 'Old Town' around the parish church and the archbishops' palace. Bourne flows are common in many areas where the Chalk lies close to an impermeable formation.

The fast-flowing and shallow waters of the Wandle, with their markedly higher average fall per mile in their upper reaches, were

Map 9

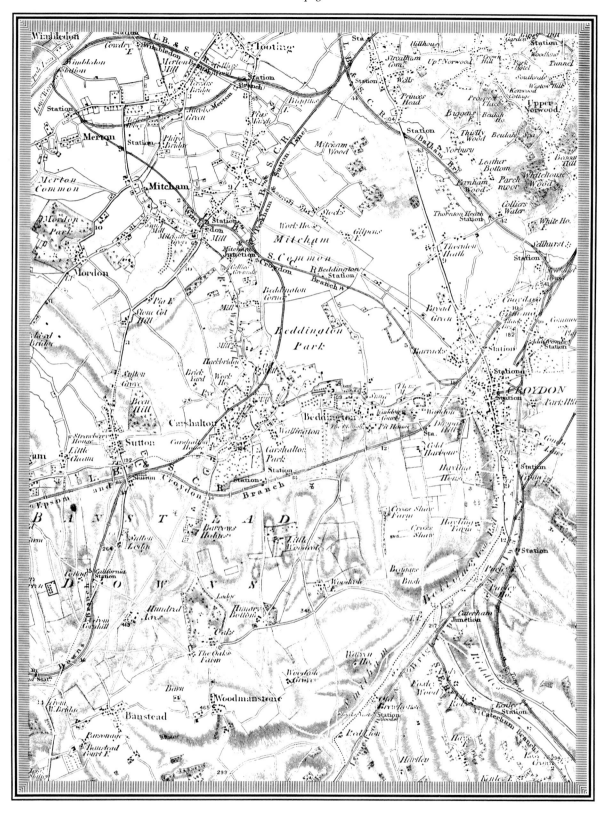

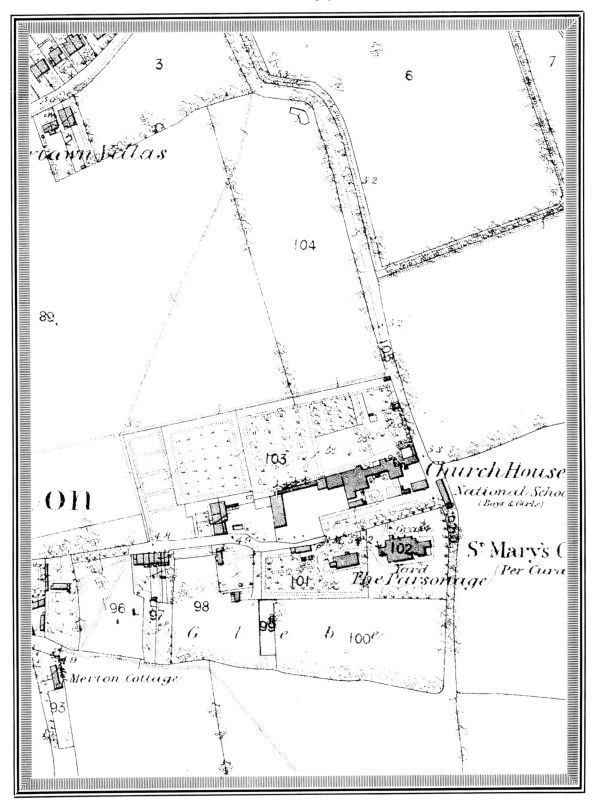

Map 9 cont.

useless for navigation but ideal for mills. Domesday Book records at least thirteen mills on the Wandle, more than half of them above Mitcham, and the row of ponds along the river from Croydon to Carshalton were used as mill ponds from a very early date. Most of the innumerable canals, cuts and sluices on the river below Hackbridge, however, seem to be of post-medieval origin. By 1600 there were no less than twenty-four corn mills on the Wandle and, at both ends of it, there were mills that ground corn continuously from the Norman conquest to the late nineteenth or early twentieth century: at Croydon, Waddon and Carshalton near the source; and the immense flour mills of Wandsworth, the lowest of which was a tide mill, near the mouth.

Detail map 9 (previous page) Admiral Nelson worshipped in the medieval parish church of St Mary, Merton, early in the nineteenth century. The immediate vicinity of the church was still totally rural late in the century but ribbon development was creeping along the north side of Kingston Road just off the northern edge of the map. Almost as close, the single-track railway from Wimbledon to Croydon had just been built.

Merton Park, as it became known, was soon to be a victim of suburbanization. John Innes of compost fame laid out an estate of large, detached villas planned in a most civilized way with much tree planting in advance of construction. The infill which followed in the 1920s and '30s was more typical of the fringe of London with much smaller houses (mainly semi-detached) on comparatively small plots.

North End, Croydon, after the introduction of horse-drawn trams in 1879 (see overleaf).

In the 1660s, the Hearth Tax Returns show that Croydon was a small town with mere 170-odd houses (apart from those that were too small to be enumerated). By 1837, there were 1667 houses and 9254 inhabitants, although the town still consisted 'chiefly of one street, nearly a mile in length'. There was a market on Saturdays and fairs on 5 July and 2 October, this last for 'horses and walnuts'. There was a large walnut tree in the grounds of Whitgift Middle School in North End until the 1960s when the school was demolished.

Croydon first saw trams in 1879. They were horse-drawn and the first route was from Thornton Heath Pond to North End (previous page and below). By 1883, other routes were available, and a through route ran from South End to Thornton Heath. The first electric tramway in the borough, using overhead supplies, was opened from Norbury to Purley on 26 September 1901. The trams last ran in 1951.

The Swan Inn, next to the Whitgift Hospital, was pulled down in 1889 and of the other buildings standing at that time at the George Street end of North End only the Whitgift Hospital of 1599 survives. The residents of the almshouses, however, still live in Whitgift's original building.

The once-moated Carew Manor, Beddington, (opposite) owes its name to the family which held it for six centuries. One of the several Nicholas Carews had his head parted from his body by Henry VIII. In about 1850, Carew Manor was purchased by the Royal Female Orphanage and largely rebuilt following a disastrous fire.

The orphants ate in the fine Tudor hall with its grand hammer-beam roof. Today the building is used by the local authority as a day school for children with special educational needs who still lunch beneath the hammer-beam roof that was there in Henry VIII's time.

The buildings in the views of Hill Road in Wimbledon (above and opposite above) are mainly the same but the road has been widened—sacrificing the roadside trees in the process. The shop and road signs have become intrusive and a very odd canopy has appeared half-way up the terrace on the left. Horse-drawn carts with, it seems, little concern about any 'rule of the road', have of course been supplanted by carefully segregated motor vehicles.

(Opposite below) The old windmill on Wimbledon Common where Robert Baden-Powell wrote Scouting for Boys in about 1908.

Carshalton Pond and Church.

Carshalton, although only 21km (23 miles) from Hyde Park Corner, could not avoid getting caught up in the economic revolution that transformed England in the nineteenth century. In 1800 Stone Court still stood as 'a handsome red-brick edifice' overlooking the canal into which the outfall from Carshalton Ponds was channelled. But the canal, after it had beautified the landscape, then drove several mills. In the following year the great house was pulled down but the mill wheels revolved ever more busily. Industry was replacing agriculture and gentlemen's residences.

Carshalton Ponds and their springs were some of the many sources of the Wandle. In the 1850s the Wandle powered eighteen corn mills, four of which were in Carshalton. The waters of the Carshalton Wandle also turned the wheels of at least six mills serving other industries (see page 68).

65

Map 10 (page 69) The Surrey Canal was made, in accordance with an Act of Parliament of 1801, from a dock at Rotherhithe to Camberwell, across the levels without a lock. It was intended originally to be carried on to the Thames at Vauxhall, but this branch was never completed. The Croydon Canal, projected at the same time, was completed and ran from the Surrey Canal at Deptford through part of Kent and Surrey to Croydon.

With the growth of London during the Industrial Revolution, a need arose to link the docks on the south and north of the Thames. The Thames Archway Company came up with a plan in 1805 for a tunnel between Rotherhithe and the Regent Canal Dock on the north of the Thames. Robert Vayce, a Cornishman whose experience of tunnelling was confined to tin mines, was engaged, but he was succeeded by Richard Trevethick. Work started in 1807 but progress was slow and finally abandoned. It was the ingenuity and resolution of the French engineer Marc Brunel (father of the railway king) which eventually led to the completion of the first tunnel under the Thames in 1843 after several disasters.

The parts of Surrey closest to London had for long been covered by suburbs of the City, and the earliest railway worked by locomotive engines in the London neighbourhood started in metropolitan Surrey. On 26 December 1838 the London and Greenwich line was opened with great ceremony. The terminus at the London end was where London Bridge station now stands. The Greenwich line was considered to be a great engineering feat, built as it was entirely on brick arches. It was undoubtedly an expensive one. The Croydon Railway followed in 1839, using the same line for a short way and then part of the bed of the old Croydon Canal. Then came the Brighton Line, which was opened in 1841.

The traffic in London Docks greatly declined after the Second World War and the Surrey Docks, opened in 1700, have been completely closed and filled in. Running from London Bridge past Tower Bridge eastwards through Bermondsey and Rotherhithe, the Surrey Docks area is, today, perhaps the most diverse within the London Docklands Enterprise Zone and offers a wide spectrum of development opportunities.

Work has already begun on the impressive London Bridge City scheme which, with the redevelopment of the historic buildings of the Courage Brewery and Butler's Wharf, is creating a strong commercial, residential and entertainment mix on the Surrey bank. New homes on sale in the area, ranging from luxurious riverside conversions such as New Concordia Wharf to newly built family units, are facing a demand that has proved far greater than expected.

Map 11 (page 70) At the time when Richmond's great deer park was being created by Charles I, many others were on the verge of extinction. The conversion of deer parks to agriculture was an important feature of the evolution of the countryside in the seventeenth and eighteenth centuries. The process is clearly illustrated at Farnham where the medieval bishops of Winchester had enclosed a deer park of 480ha (1200 acres) to the north and west of the castle. In 1696 an Act of Parliament 'disparked' the Old Park and almost 360ha (900 acres) of land were opened up to new farms. The landscape of early eighteenth-century colonization to the north-west of Farnham is disclosed by the names of its three farms—Upper Old Park, Middle Old Park and Lower Old Park. The formal rectangular pattern of fields and the long narrow planted spinneys suggest a landscape that was shaped according to the ideas of the eighteenth century. In Farnham Castle Park, however, a relic of the medieval landscape remains—the lonely trees and gentle contours unencumbered by fences speak of a different period of landscape history.

*Comparison with the picture on page 73 shows how
little this part of Compton has changed in the last one
hundred years.*

The most noticeable difference between this area of Carshalton Ponds today and in the late nineteenth century (page 64) is the loss of Queen's Well, the white house seen by the church, which was named after the spring by its front gate to which a totally spurious legend about Anne Boleyn had become attached.

Map 10

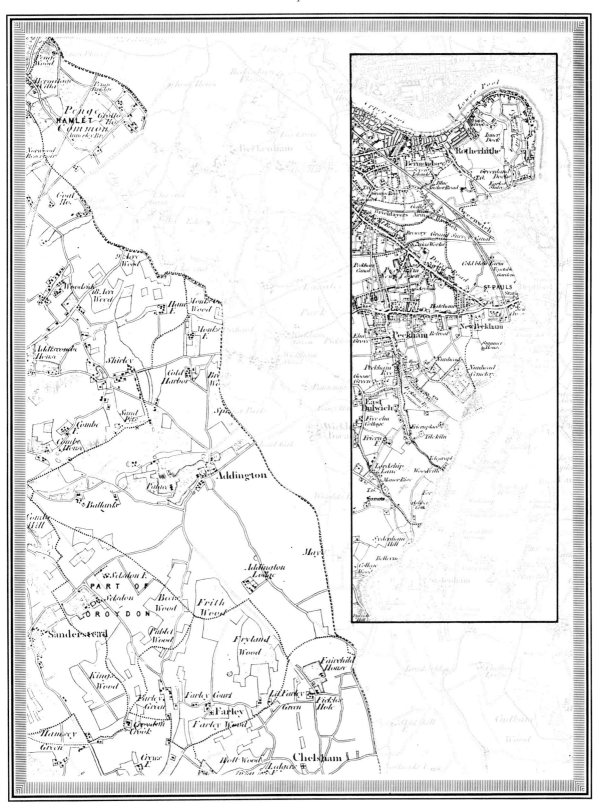

Map 11

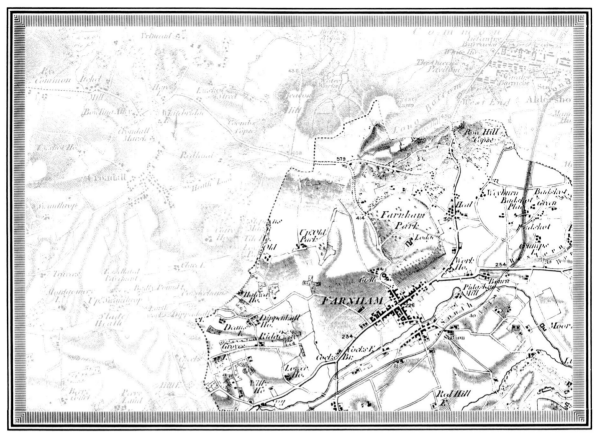

Map 11 cont.

From the late seventeenth to the nineteenth century, Farnham was the centre of some of the most advanced agriculture in Surrey. The first Act of Parliament for enclosure in Surrey was a private Act of the eighth year of Queen Anne for the enclosure of the disparked land at Farnham. By the end of the century, Farnham was famous for its hops and this was the only aspect of Surrey farming of which Arthur Young approved in 1796 during his *Six Weeks' Tour of the South of England.*

For many centuries, the danger of fire in towns largely composed of timber-framed houses was a very serious one. The surprisingly modern aspect of many ancient towns is often due to their having been swept by fire as, for instance, the old market town of Buckingham in 1725. To the result of fire or the fear of it we often owe the rebuilding in eighteenth-

century brick of many country towns, and the tall fronts and mellow red colouring of the later houses lend a distinguished air to Farnham's West and Castle Streets. Fashion followed and many timber-framed houses were refronted in brick for appearances' sake.

Farnham had the premier market for wheat in the country and in the 1700s its corn market was said to be second only to London. Its timber-framed market hall was built when Elizabeth I was on the throne and stood at the bottom end of Castle Street until 1866. Had it survived another hundred years, it would undoubtedly have been treasured as one of the town's many important reminders of its past.

Map 12

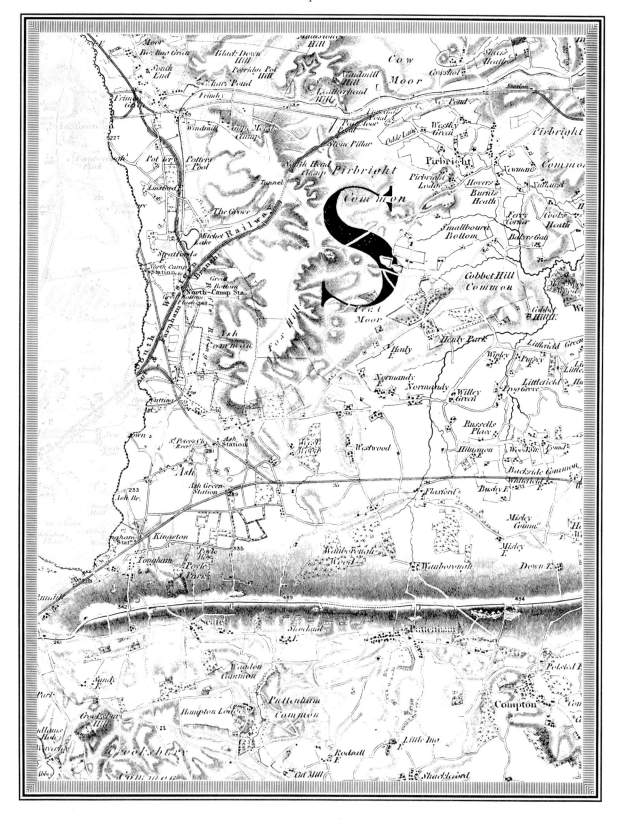

Map 12 Through the centre of the county west of Guildford runs the sharp spine of the Hog's Back, dividing the greensand heath country to the south from the Tertiary heathland to the north. South of the Hog's Back there is a lower tract of country coinciding with the outcrop of softer rocks in the Greensand. The most important of these are the Folkestone Beds, consisting mainly of soft, deep yellow sand which turns grey on weathering—the horticulturalist's 'silver sand'. The soils associated with these beds are cruelly sterile and dry out quickly and, for this reason, much of the outcrop has been left as commons and open heaths with bracken, bilberry, heather and gorse in competition with occasional groups of silver birch, isolated oak trees and self-seeded conifers. The commons of south-west Surrey, which form some of the largest and most popular open areas close to London, nearly all occur on the Folkestone Sands outcrop.

The proximity to London of the Tertiary heathlands north of the Hog's Back was to make it the scene of military exercises and rifle competitions in the late nineteenth century. Inevitably, this became accompanied by the growth of military depots, particularly noticeable near the county boundary by Aldershot—the prototype of all army towns.

Compton village is one of the prettiest in Surrey and busy with tourists on fine summer Sundays (see page 67). Its church contains a unique two-storeyed chancel and a rare wooden balustrade, both of Norman date. On a hill overlooking the village is a memorial chapel to the artist Frederick Watts in, also rare, art nouveau terracotta.

Map 13

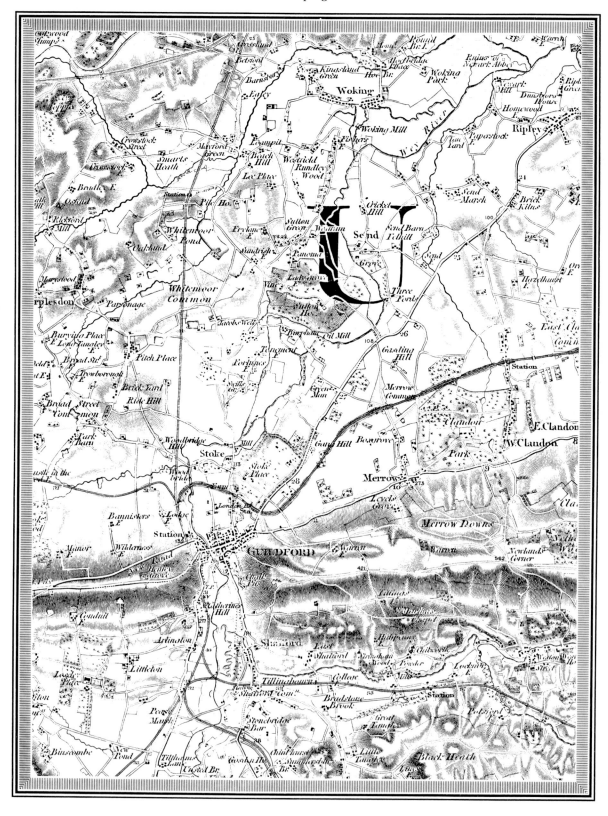

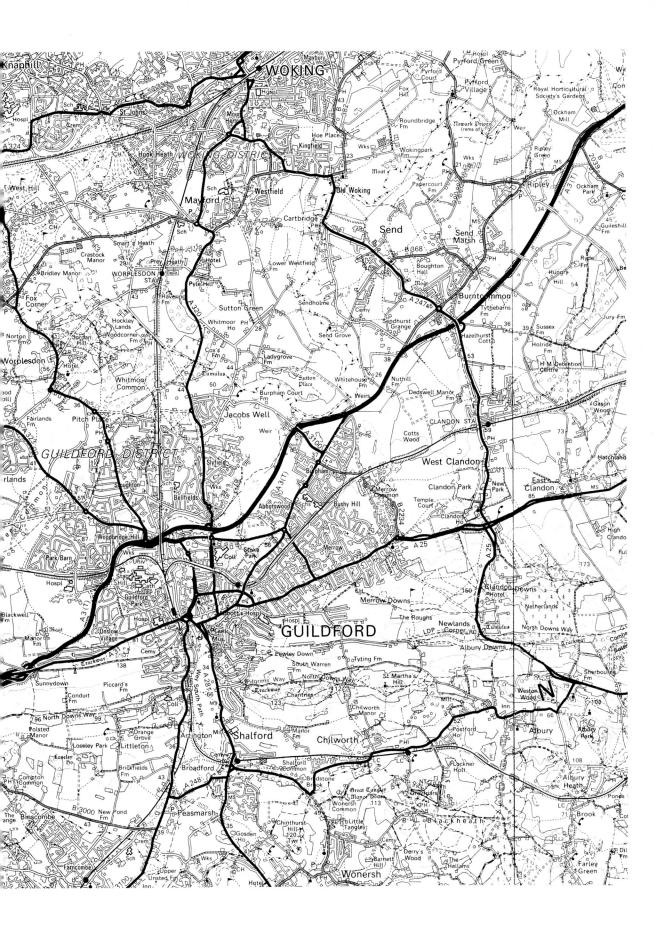

Map 13 and modern map 13 (overleaf) Sir Richard Weston of Sutton Place brought Surrey into the van of agricultural progress when, in 1645, he introduced clover from Flanders or Brabant. In 1650, in a book styled *Directions for the Improvement of Barren Lands*, he recommended the cultivation of turnips, anticipating by seventy years their introduction into Norfolk by Lord Townshend. Turnips had, in fact, been known in England as a garden vegetable long before this but there is reason to suppose that it was in Surrey that they were first extensively cultivated.

In 1769 Arthur Young, during his *Six Weeks' Tour of Southern Britain*, found the rotation of crops near Guildford to be 'unscientific'. It was (1) fallow; (2) wheat; (3) spring corn; (4) clover; (5) wheat; (6) beans, peas or oats. Three quarters of wheat was, he says, considered a middling good crop. The ploughing was done by teams of four horses or of four, six or eight oxen. Nearly all 'judicious persons' consulted by Young during his tour preferred to use oxen but horse teams were more common by ten to one. Plough oxen had quite disappeared from Surrey by the nineteenth century.

At the end of the eighteenth century, land near and south of Guildford let at from 10s to 15s an acre. Between Guildford and Ripley, the higher rate prevailed. Wages were 1s 2d per day in winter, 1s 4d in spring, 2s to 2s 6d during harvest. Prices were mutton 4½d per pound; beef, 4d; bread, 2d; butter, 7d. Rents were lower than near London, wages a trifle lower but prices much the same.

Until recent times, Guildford and Kingston upon Thames were the two principal towns in Surrey apart from Southwark, which really functioned as a suburb of London. Guildford was the county town but, in the nineteenth century, the increasing attractions of London meant that Guildford was unable to maintain itself in this role. The home of the quarter sessions was transferred to Newington although the Spring Assizes were held at Kingston and the Summer Assizes at Guild-ford. After the formation of the new county of London in 1889, various towns claimed the right to be the seat of the county's administration, but the new County Hall was built at Kingston.

Guildford grew through the nineteenth century (its population was around 10,000 in the 1880s) but it was not until the late 1920s that the town exploded into the modern satellite role to London that it now firmly fulfils. In the late nineteenth century Roger Fry, a leading art critic who had built a villa near Guildford, half apologized to his visitors for a countryside spotted with so many 'gentlemanly residences'. Since then, the industrial development and residential growth of Guildford both before and since the Second World War has spreadeagled the town across the landscape into a sprawling mass.

--- ◇◇◇ ---

Detail map 13 The late nineteenth-century plan of Guildford still showed, on either side of the High Street, the long, narrow plots that went back to medieval times. The plots extended to North Street to the north and South and Castle Streets to the south, successors to the original ditches which demarcated the town when it was first laid out, probably in the tenth century.

The railway came to Guildford in 1845 and caused an expansion of industry in the town centre, and the growth of suburbs. The historic fabric of the core was largely unaffected, however, for another hundred years. Pressure between the wars led to the construction of the first bypass and there was an abortive proposal in 1938 to widen the High Street by demolishing one whole side. Since 1950, however, a new traffic system has been laid out in the town centre involving the destruction of many interesting buildings and the construction of two river crossings north of the old bridge, which has been closed to all but pedestrians. The new and much wider roads occupy a substantial amount of the town centre and have been accompanied by a shift

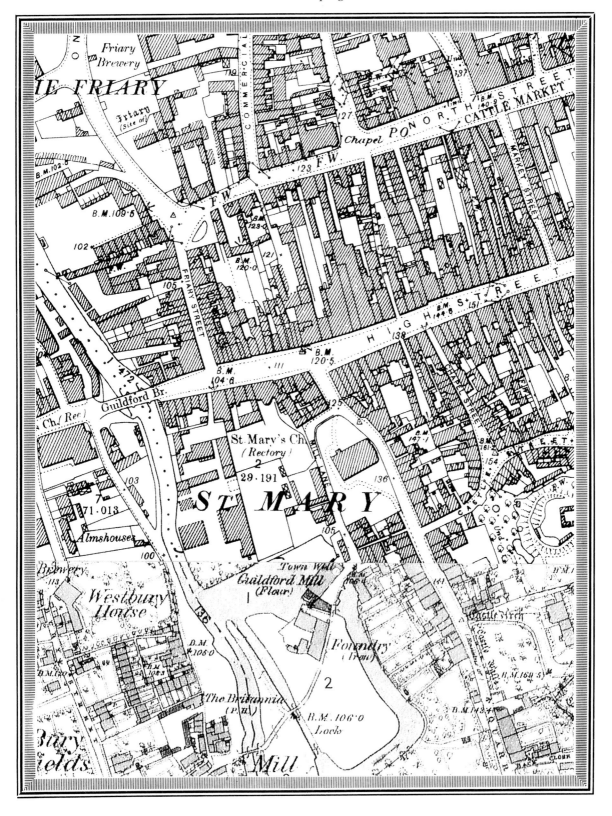

Detail map 13 cont.
from industry (the Friary Brewery) to shopping malls and offices. There has been a dramatic amalgamation of property units both near the new roads and on both sides of the High Street. The central retail distribution and administrative functions of the town centre have become paramount.

Before 1960, eleven buildings in Guildford High Street listed under the 1947 Town and Country Planning Act as being of architectural merit or historic interest had disappeared. Among these was the White Lion, a former coaching inn with a long and distinguished stuccoed façade (opposite). It had been demolished in 1957 to make way for a wholly undistinguished rectangular box built to house a branch of Woolworths.

The Woolworth building did not last long, and its site, together with adjacent properties stretching back into North Street, was redeveloped in 1984–5 as White Lion Walk—a shopping arcade in the contemporary 'Post Modernist' manner (above).

79

Guildford High Street in the late nineteenth century

In 1896, the Society for the Protection of Ancient Buildings expressed anxiety about the future of Guildford's High Street (previous page and above) and urged the citizens of the town to form a 'watching committee'. Individual buildings have been picked off in the intervening decades and little of interest remains below first-floor level. There is little doubt that the survival of what remains of Guildford's architectural heritage is due in no small part to the activities of the Old Guildford Society (1887–1903) and the present Guildford Society (formed in 1936 and still flourishing).

Guildford's North Street (above and overleaf) runs on the line of the medieval boundary ditch of the town but its width betrays its early use as a market. A century ago it was used as a livestock market. Now, daily use as a street market maintains its historic role but the sheep have gone. The church spire in the background in 1900 has been replaced by Barclays Bank.

Surrey watermills were often large wooden structures of great beauty like Newark Mill, near Ripley, seen here in 1903 but tragically destroyed by fire in the 1970s, or the smaller Castle Mill, Dorking which is still preserved, albeit at considerable change in character arising from its conversion to residential use. The site of the mill-race of Newark Mill is now occupied by an attractive riverside garden.

Map 14

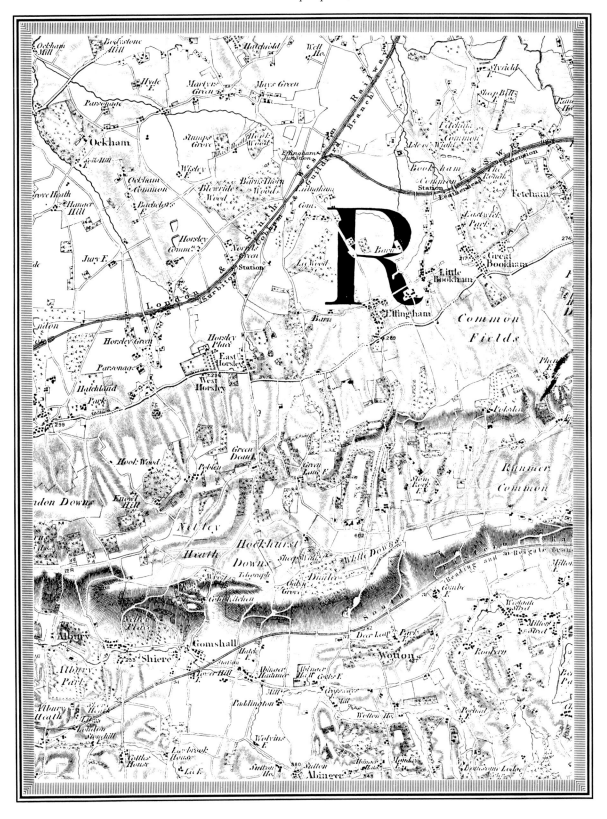

Map 14 (previous page) The Tillingbourne Valley and the Downs above it are among the finest and most delicate landscapes in Surrey. In the seventeenth century, the Tillingbourne was an industrial river, and the industry helped to pay for elaborate gardens by John Evelyn at Wotton and Albury. The industry lingered through the eighteenth century but, by the time of the first Ordnance Survey, apart from the tannery at Gomshall, it was largely confined to the stretch downstream of Albury Park (see map on page 74). Evelyn's plantations of Leith Hill were growing lustily and were influencing other landowners.

In the nineteenth century, the rambler and hiker discovered the joys of walking in Surrey with the help of successively improved editions of the Ordnance Survey one-inch map. Because of the variety of unspoilt scenery, Surrey then offered the best walking within reach of a day's excursion from London. Late Victorian men of letters were great walkers: Carlyle, Robert Louis Stevenson, Hilaire Belloc and George Meredith were all devotees of Surrey rambling.

The best known walking society of the time was that called the Sunday Tramps. This group regularly took a day's walk in Surrey, and Meredith recorded one of their outings in 1880. Leslie Stephenson was the founder of the group, and has been called the 'patron saint of ramblers', with the triangle of walking country bounded by Guildford, Leatherhead and Leith Hill his shrine. Another distinguished Surrey rambler was 'Walker Miles' (Edmund Seybang Taylor) who wrote numerous walking guides. He is buried in Godstone churchyard and memorialized at the top of Leith Hill tower.

This area remains as popular today and, of course, the motor car has brought it within reach of an increasing number of people. The unique value of this landscape is protected by current planning policies and it is to be fervently hoped that it will always remain so.

Map 15 There were once commons, or wastes, associated with most Surrey villages but, from the late Middle Ages on, many of these have been gradually eroded by enclosure and squatting. By the late eighteenth century, enclosure was at full tide. Between 1794 and 1809, 120ha (300 acres) of common were enclosed at Penge; 140ha (350 acres) at Croydon; the same amount at Ewell; 450ha (1100 acres), including open fields, at Fetcham and Bookham; 60ha (150 acres) at Clandon; 320ha (800 acres) at Peasemarsh. In all, more than 2000ha (5000 acres) of commons and open fields were enclosed in the county during the first forty years of George III, but the map shows that open fields still existed in Surrey in 1816.

Before this, largely in the eighteenth century, the landscape of the Mickleham Gap had been turned into one great park-scape. The Lockes of Norbury were pre-eminent but fine houses and parks were also established at Denbies, Camilla Lacey, Juniper Hall, Mickleham Hall, Polesden Lacey and Deepdene. Sheridan lived at Polesden Lacey, Fanny Burney at Camilla Lacey and Thomas Hope at Deepdene.

By 1900, the private homes of the wealthy in this 'highly favoured county' were turning the heart of Surrey into the fringe of outwardly developing London. Along the North Downs were the residences of persons who had amassed wealth from shipping, banking, coal and 'contracting'. Public concern was expressed for the summit ridge itself, and in 1912 the *Spectator* said, 'We have now reached the stage when the further placing of houses along the ridge can only spoil and disfigure the whole.'

In the years immediately before 1914, many landowners were perturbed by the budgets and land taxes introduced by the then Chancellor of the Exchequer, Mr Lloyd George, and were anxious to sell some of their land—especially at the prices obtainable for building lots. Public reaction was dramatic and was easily harnessed but an incalculable

Map 15

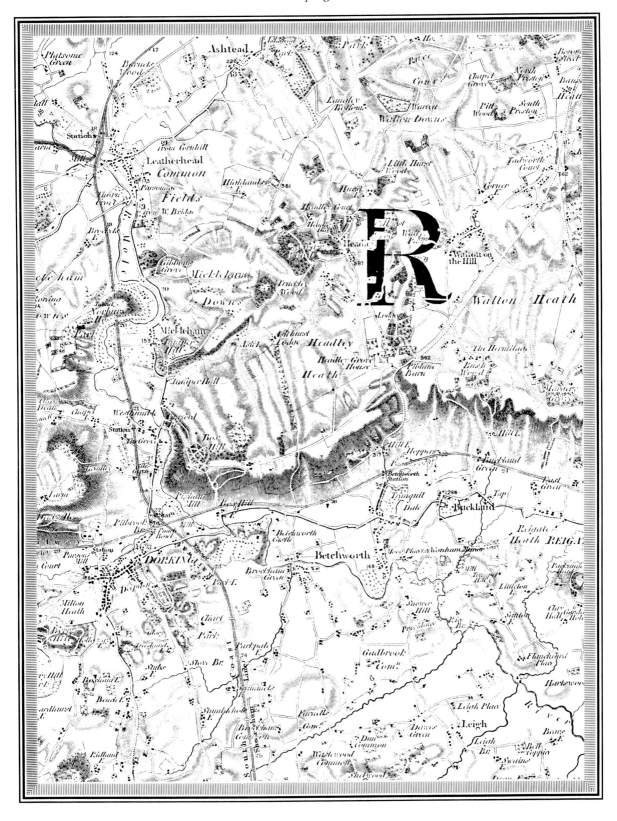

The fire station (with clock) at Leatherhead housed the engine; the horses were stabled nearby. The fire station itself has now gone but many of the houses in Gravel Hill (behind) are still there. The Post Office has moved but the building survives.

Map 15 cont.

debt is owed to the generosity of individuals who presented land to the National Trust or who supported appeals for money to purchase land for the nation at, for example, Colley and Box Hills.

It is estimated that today at least two million Londoners look to Surrey as their primary centre of recreation or pass through it annually on their way to the coast. As a result, several Surrey beauty spots such as Box Hill, Leith Hill and Frensham Common were suffering from severe over-use, even before the M25 motorway opened.

Map 16 and modern map 16 (overleaf) South of the Chalk of the North Downs is the Gault Clay. Throughout the length of its outcrop, this is a relatively thin formation but, when fully developed, it forms a valley of considerable landscape importance. East of Dorking, the name Holmesdale is normally given to the valley.

Between Godstone and Betchworth, the Gault Clay is replaced increasingly by the sandy and calcareous beds known as the Upper Greensand. Around Merstham, these beds form a distinct bench due to the presence of the rock known as firestone which is hard enough to resist erosion. In the past, the pale grey 'firestone' has been exploited for use in important buildings in the London Basin in medieval times and for building local houses and churches in the late nineteenth century. A softer layer, the 'hearthstone', was mined until 1963 for use as cleaning blocks.

East of Reigate the recurrence of the chert and harder sands in the Lower Greensand beds is reflected by the reappearance of the greensand ridge. Close to the Folkestone Beds of the Lower Greensand lies the narrow and discontinuous belt of the outcrop of the Sandgate Beds. These are mostly loamy sands which are easily eroded. In the Nutfield and Bletchingley area the Sandgate Beds have workable deposits of Fuller's Earth which

have been exploited at least since medieval times and were in great demand in the cloth industry, both locally and far afield. Although very little of the Fuller's Earth is now used for its traditional purpose of removing grease from wool, it is still in demand and the peace of Bletchingley is threatened by a proposal to open a huge new quarry.

Reigate was first recorded as *Churchefelle* in the eleventh century when it was probably an area of scattered settlements. It was given to William de Warenne on his creation as Earl of Surrey and soon after is found under its present name. Until the eighteenth century the road system of Reigate was centred on the old junction of West Street, Nutley Lane, London Lane (now London Road) and the High Street. Its population in 1801 was a modest 2000, including the surrounding district.

The Surrey Iron Railway from Wandsworth to Croydon (see maps on pages 32 and 56), established under an Act of Parliament of 1802, was so successful that it was extended to Merstham, although a proposal to extend the railway still further to the stone quarries at Godstone was never put into practice. There was a further project for connecting the Wey and Arun Canal, by a branch through Horsham, with the terminus of the railway at Merstham. It is possible that in this way additional traffic might have been encouraged but it is hardly surprising that the scheme never got any further. The railway between Croydon and Merstham was itself not successful. The gradients were too steep for the horses and the amount of traffic did not justify the capital invested. Steam power, even by fixed engines, was not considered. The railway was bought out by the London and Brighton Railway Company in 1838 and the site of the terminus at Merstham is now ironically buried beneath the carriageway of the M23.

Redhill was created around the railway station, which was rebuilt on the present site in 1849 when the Ashford and Reading lines had been completed. The railway company laid

Map 16

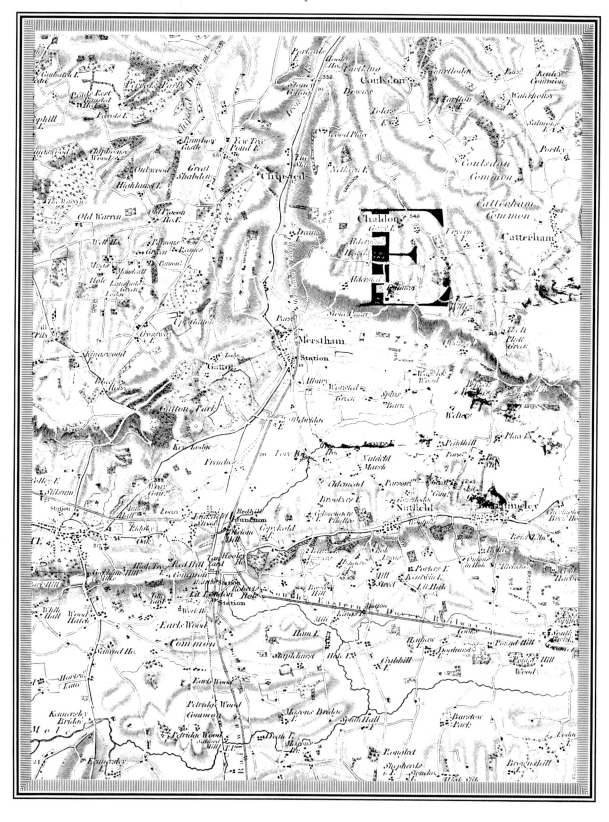

A mechanical reaper in use at Colley Hill, Reigate, in 1906 (see overleaf).

When the first edition of Ordnance Survey maps was published, harvesting was carried out with sickle and scythe (opposite). Mechanical reapers were introduced in the late Victorian era and the picture on page 94 shows one in use in the fields below Colley Hill, Reigate, in about 1906. They were still horse-drawn until well after the end of the First World War, Colley Hill is still a much valued part of the Surrey Green Belt (see map on page 93), although the tower block just visible on the horizon indicates that Reigate is not far away.

Map 16 and modern map 16 cont.

out Station Road and the road eastwards to the top of Redstone Hill. By 1860, a small settlement called Warwick Town was established. Redhill grew rapidly throughout the latter part of the nineteenth century, thriving as a centre of commerce because of the railway.

The Brighton line was opened in 1841 and was followed by the Dover Railway for which the Act had been passed in 1836. It was completed from Redhill to Ashford in 1842. The trains ran out of London on the Croydon line and paid to it a fixed charge of one shilling per passenger.

The engineers had originally planned to use the Mole Gap through the Downs and the corresponding Shoreham Gap in the South Downs as offering the easiest route for the Brighton line, and the line was planned to run by Epsom and Leatherhead. Some landowners near Leatherhead objected violently to the invasion of their fields, and employed a clever advocate to persuade Brighton that a line in this direction would bring Worthing as near to London as Brighton itself, which would interfere with Brighton's one great advantage. The argument was forcible and prevailed. The direct route to Brighton was adopted.

On the line of the M23 and the London to Brighton railway, the dam of the Green Belt has been breached by a busy transport, residential and industrial corridor. Building is virtually continuous from Croydon to Gatwick with only a short break between Coulsdon and Merstham—and even this intermission has the 1930s housing development of Hooley in the middle of it and the 'Dutch' village a short distance further north.

———◇◇◇———

Detail Map 16 (overleaf) The landscape round Quarry Dean, Merstham, shown on this 1:2500 map has been affected by the construction of the M23. Quarry Dean was the site of stone quarrying and mining in the Upper Greensand from medieval times (it was known as Querrepitden in 1528) to the nineteenth century. The two 'Old Chalk Pits' marked on the map to the south-east of Quarry Dean were really entries to mine galleries, and motorway construction in the 1970s was greatly impeded by the need to backfill miles of these galleries.

The Croydon, Merstham and Godstone Railway (an extension of the Surrey Iron Railway) reached here in 1804, encouraged

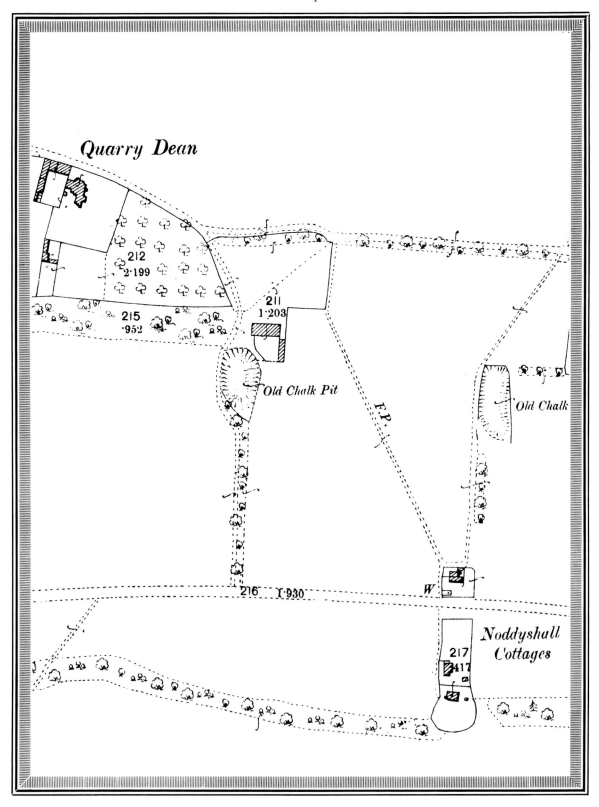

Quarry Dean

212
2·199

215
·952

211
1·203

Old Chalk Pit

F.P.

Old Chalk

216   I·930

W

Noddyshall
Cottages

217
·417

Detail map 16 cont.

by the local contracting partnership of William Jolliffe and Edward Banks which contributed to the building of London Bridge between 1827 and 1830. The terminus of the railway had been in plot no. 211 on this map. A chalk pit just beyond the north-west corner was run by a succession of different firms and reached gigantic proportions before its closure in 1956. The pit was then filled with domestic refuse from Croydon and eventually grassed over shortly before the construction of the motorway.

Redhill is one of several 'railway towns' in Surrey. It started life named Warwick Town after the widow of the fourth Lord Monson but, as the undistinguished terraces of the 1860s and 1870s spread across the surrounding meadows, the name of the old manor of Redhill prevailed.

Built in 1860 in the eclectic style of its time, Redhill's Market Hall (above) was demolished in the early 1980s to make way for a shopping mall with civic theatre and library above—after more than a quarter of a century of argument over the development of this and adjacent sites (see page 114).

Brighton Road, Redhill, was on a branch of the London to Brighton turnpike (overleaf and page 115), made in 1815 to bypass Reigate Hill but, when the railway was built in 1841, the road must have become peaceful and nearly deserted until the town of Redhill grew up. Even in 1906 it was still possible to park a cart right across the carriageway, although the shape of things to come was presaged in the garage sign and advertisement for 'motor spirit'.

Map 17

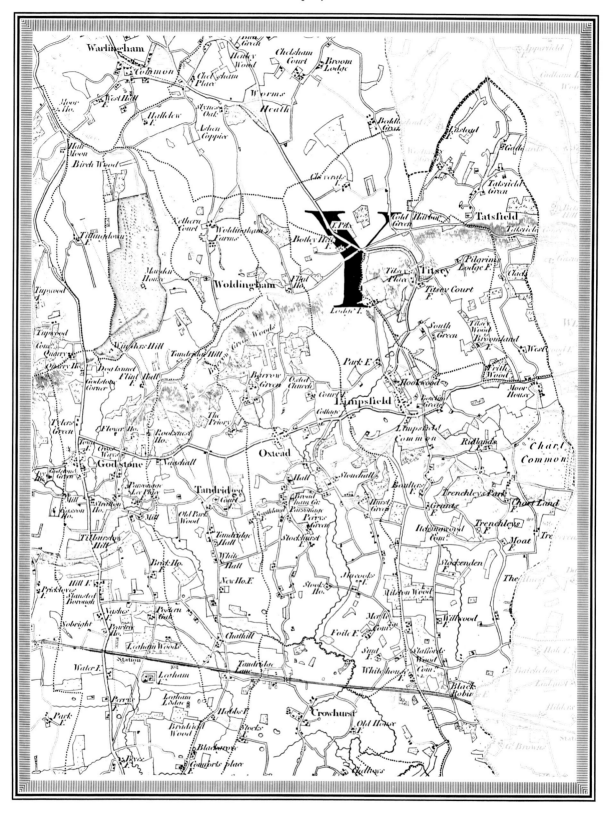

Map 17 and modern map 17 (pages 102 and 103) In East Surrey, the formation which makes the biggest impression on the scenery is the Chalk. Although fairly uniform in composition, the outcrop shows great variation in width largely due to the changing dip of the beds. This decreases eastwards. The height of the chalk crest also increases eastwards and, close to Tatsfield, it reaches its greatest height of 270m (886 feet) above mean sea level.

Because of its facility for swallowing surface water, which gives it a considerable degree of resistance to erosion, the Chalk everywhere presents a steep scarp overlooking the Vale of Holmesdale to the south. It has a broken appearance as a result of the presence of shallow, armchair-shaped coombes. These erosional features probably came into being during the last Ice Age.

A string of commons follows the outcrop of the Lower Greensand through both Kent and Surrey. At Limpsfield, we find the Chart and Limpsfield Common. The place-name 'Chart' occurs almost thirty times in Surrey and Kent and describes rough and uncultivated land, overgrown with gorse, broom and bracken. Nowhere else in the British Isles do we find this Old English term and, even in Kent and Surrey, it is limited to the outcrop of the Lower Greensand. The 'certs' or charts first appear in the documentary record with the Anglo-Saxon charters of the seventh and eighth centuries. The fact that the charts can be traced back as place-names to the seventh century suggests that the open heaths were already in existence at the time of the Anglo-Saxon settlements. But it is also true that, without the interference of man and his grazing animals, the heaths of the greensand hills would soon be covered by insidiously expanding woods of birch and pine. In many places we can see that scrubby close-growing birch and pine have invaded the commons in the past half century, with the decline of grazing and the abandonment of common rights.

That any rural landscape has survived at all in Surrey is largely due to the concept of the Metropolitan Green Belt, the primary barrier erected against the inexorable advance of London, which developed out of the voluntary preservation of Surrey's countryside before the Second World War. The Green Belt has had a profound influence on the present character of Surrey, but the question for the future is whether the concept can be maintained. Already, the Green Belt has provided an easy corridor for the London Orbital Motorway (M25).

Surrey's historic dependence on London has been emphasized by the construction of the M25. This road has been particularly difficult to fit into the gentle flowing Surrey countryside on account of its width and vast intersections. 'Landscaping' of the motorway has been attempted, but it will be several years before the trees mature so that this can be assessed. Any motorway requires service stations along its length and one such has been proposed for Clacket Wood, on the county boundary. This is a fine area of ancient woodland and the proposal has generated much opposition but, as the M25 passes through much sensitive landscape, it may well be that no location can be found that will be acceptable to road users and transportation planners as well as to local residents and amenity societies.

This chalk pit near Betchworth is one of many on the ridge which runs across this part of east Surrey and into Kent.

Old Oxted (overleaf and page 116), like many Surrey villages, consists of one narrow and battered street: in this case, it runs uphill from east to west. In 1890 the High Street was poorly surfaced and the footpath ill-defined, but today hard-edged kerbs and road lines have changed the atmosphere.

Thursley lies nearly three miles north of Hindhead on the edge of the heath. It is Thor's ley or Thor's field, and has memories of the pagan deities. Thor lies in local legends, particularly at the strange conical hills of the Devil's Jumps.

Thursley Common once rang with the sounds of hammers and its string of hammer ponds are still full of water. The Weald has a long history of iron works and in the sixteenth and seventeenth centuries was the centre of Britain's iron industry.

William Cobbett, riding from Hampshire or Sussex early in the nineteenth century, used to make Thursley his regular stopping place. But he did not come over Hindhead, for he detested the wild unfertile heath. He preferred to ride through woods or between fields.

The Red Lion was an inn on the turnpike built in 1826 (see previous page), a few years before Cobbett's death. But the toll-road that Cobbett hated so much has now been bypassed with a dual carriageway and the Red Lion finds itself on a backwater. Trade has gone and the inn is now a private house. The large shed on the right is clearly older than it looks, and is now a garage.

Maps 18, 19 and modern map 19 (opposite and overleaf) The outstanding feature of south-west Surrey is the magnificent greensand hill of Hindhead with the remarkable Devil's Punchbowl. In the eighteenth century, Hindhead was the feared haunt of highwaymen and other thieves—with a gibbet to warn those who might be tempted to take up the trade.

The Punchbowl was the home of the Broom Squires. At the opening of the nineteenth century, on the heaths from near Dorking to the borders of Hampshire, the people were rough and untaught, frequently far from their parish churches and with formerly few or no resident gentry among them (the taste for picturesque residences only arises when such residences can be readily brought within touch of civilization). They were wholly given over to irregular means of livelihood and were the real descendants of the 'stout vagabonds' whom Elizabeth I's government had impressed for soldiers. Forest industries, such as charcoal-burning, broom-

Map 18

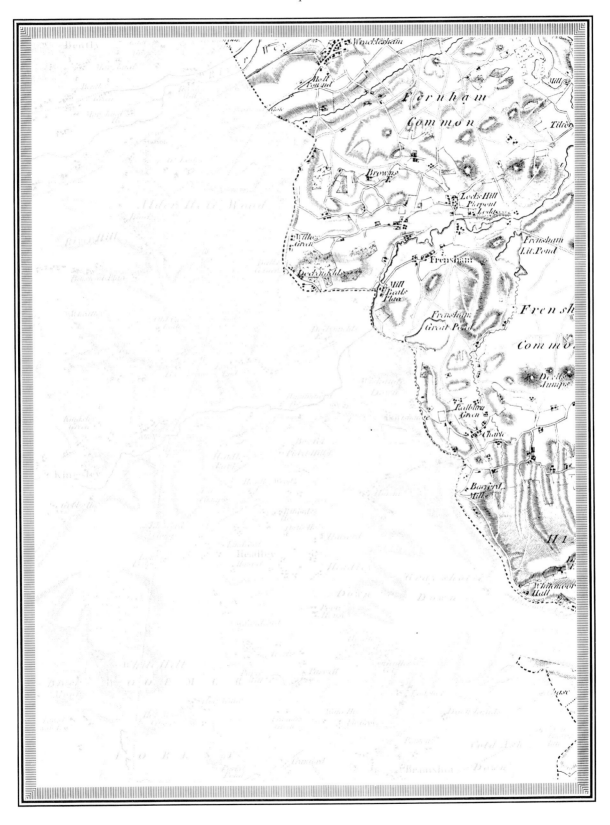

Map 19

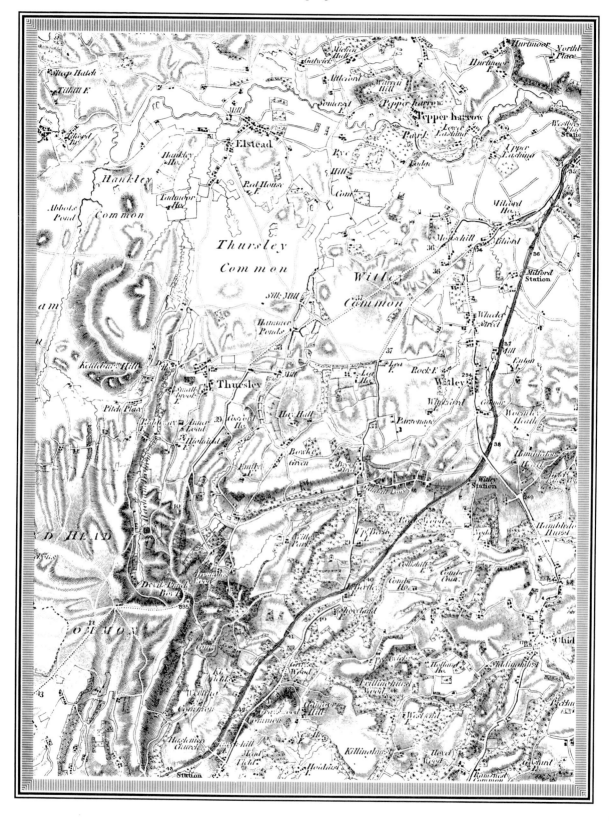

The site of Redhill's nineteenth-century market hall today (see page 99).

*Brighton Road, Redhill today. Since the early picture
(page 100) was taken in 1906, the road has been
widened, reducing the size of the gardens on the right.
Very few of the buildings have survived.*

Oxted is still recognizable when compared with the picture of 1890 (page 106), and has become more peaceful since the creation of a bypass and the M25.

making and turf-cutting, enabled them to live where the proceeds of husbandry on the sandy soils were barely sufficient for such a purpose even when supplemented by poaching in all its aspects, shooting, fishing, snaring and smuggling.

Cobbett hated the infertility of Hindhead and avoided the place as much as he could. But amid the greensand heaths there is a narrow strip of country that runs from Churt to Thursley that has been favoured for farming for a long time. Here, there is a belt of arable land seldom more than half a mile wide which contains eight large farms along its three-mile length.

With the coming of the railway, the area was opened up to both the rambler and the commuter. Late in the century, the spread of unpleasantly obtrusive villas in formerly undiscovered parts of Surrey represented a most serious onslaught on the landscape. George Meredith became increasingly concerned in the 1890s about the 'hectoring of lovely country by hideous villas', although an earlier visit by William Morris to Witley had left him surprised at it being 'amazingly free from anything Cockney-based'. However, the growing villadom of urban interlopers on Hindhead repelled Morris.

As on the North Downs and Leith Hill, an incalculable debt is owed here to the generosity of individuals who have since presented land to the National Trust or who have supported appeals for money to purchase land for the nation. Milford and Witley Commons were preserved from development by their gift to the nation by the architect Thackery Turner in 1921. Hindhead was preserved by means of a public appeal.

———◇◇◇———

Map 20 (overleaf) East of Hindhead, the clay vale of the Low Weald stretches into the distance. Nearby, the landscape is more undulating than in the Low Weald further east, largely as a result of beds of limestone and sandstone within the clay. In places where the thin sandstone or limestone beds outcrop, the soils are lighter and under arable cultivation. It is noticeable that, in the Low Weald of south-west Surrey, all the farmsteads with arguably early place-names are on such outcrops or on periglacial soils. Close by Chiddingfold, a sandstone bed was of great importance to the medieval and early post-medieval glass-making industry. The sandstone has also been much valued in the past as a building stone, particularly the Horsham Stone which splits readily into thin slabs and was therefore used for roofing and paving. The clay beds themselves were once extensively used for brick-making.

Before metalled roads and the railways were driven through the area, conditions were treacherous under foot, especially in winter. In the Weald, a stone causeway would run from the road up to the door of farmhouse or cottage because in wet weather the path would otherwise be almost impassable.

The Wey Navigation was extended to Godalming in the late eighteenth century and the Arun Navigation had been extended to Wisborough Green. The Wey and Arun Canal—marked on the map as the Surrey and Sussex Canal—formed a connecting link between the two systems—thus providing an inland route between London and Portsmouth. The canal had been built under the pressure of the French Wars but did not open until the year after Waterloo. It always suffered from lack of water in its summit level and was not a commercial success. It was closed down in 1871.

As late as the 1880s, remoter parts of Surrey retained, at least in outward appearance, the way of life of centuries before. People were often still paid for services in kind; the village stocks still stood on the green; each farm still possessed its own lime kiln. Wealden farms and cottages were normally roofed in the flaggy Horsham Stone and, south and west of Dorking, many of the older houses still have Horsham slab roofs. These heavy slabs,

Map 20

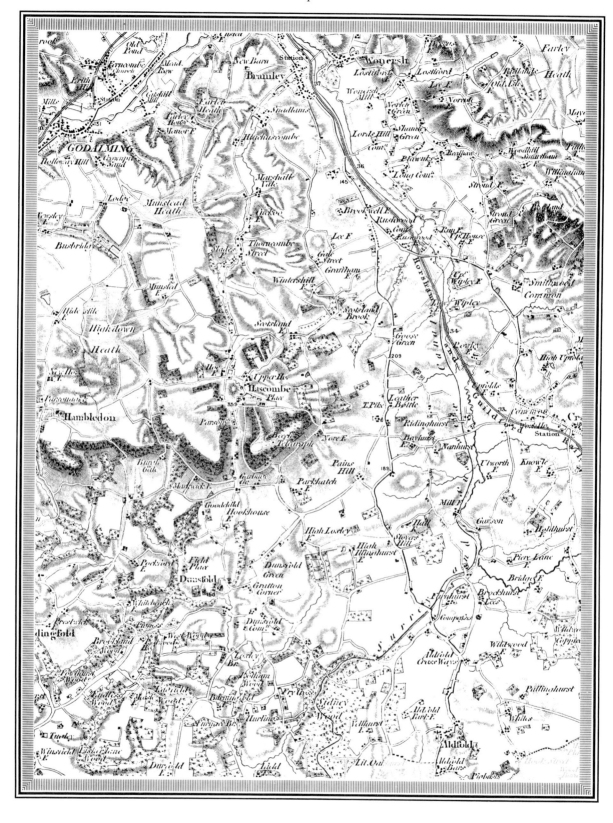

Map 20 cont.

delightfully mellowed by weathering and moss, are so durable that many existing buildings still retain their original roofing, as is indicated by a liberal amount of soot on its underside, derived from the hall fire of the farmstead, before the 'lofting over' of the hall during the Great Rebuilding of the sixteenth and seventeenth centuries. Today, Horsham slabs are expensive and, where roofs require renewing, it is usual to retain slabs only on the most visible side of the building.

In some ways the least spoiled of Surrey's towns, Godalming retains much of charm. The perspectives vary continuously along its curving High Street (above and overleaf) and there are many individual buildings of interest although, inevitably, little of historic interest remains below first-floor level. Most entertaining among the buildings in the High Street is the early nineteenth-century Market Hall, a shapely stuccoed building with an open arcaded ground floor and surmounted by the 'pepper pot' just visible in the background of the photograph.

Map 21 (overleaf) South-west of Dorking, the country was said to be the haunt of 'stubborn and uncivil people' around 1800. About Holmbury and Ewhurst Hills, the population was of the worst type of heath-men, or heathers (pronounced as in *heathen*). If a sheep stolen from a farm in more settled neighbourhoods were traced in this direction, all would abandon pursuit: the people of the district, it was known, would hang together to conceal the theft and the criminals.

Smuggling was common. Cargoes were run upon the south coast and hidden in convenient places near the South Downs. During the French wars, brandy came across the Channel in large rowing boats on calm, foggy nights. From Sussex, smuggled goods were brought on horses another stage of their journey to the Surrey hills and concealed there until they could be brought to London. There are still cottages with big cellars running under the hills, intended for the storage of contraband.

It is easy in Surrey to detect the character of the Victorian landed estates, and there are several around Abinger and Holmbury. From a distance, clumps of conifers such as Calabrian pine, Norwegian spruce and noble fir are reminders of the vanished way of life as well as contributions to the landscape. Closer to, winding, laurel-girt public roads conceal, with the decorum of a drive, wide sweeps of raked and watered gravel leading to red-gabled villas. Thicker hedgerows, well-kept luxuriant woodland, neat 'model' fields and farm buildings were also characteristics that sometimes survive. The spread of such suburban property forms was, however, obliterating for ever the old agricultural Surrey.

In the nineteenth century, Leith Hill and the lands around it were largely in the hands of large landowners with little desire to sell. But the rising prices of building land produced forces which were difficult to resist. The first steps in efforts to preserve Leith Hill, threatened by speculative building, were taken in 1929 when land was purchased from

Map 21

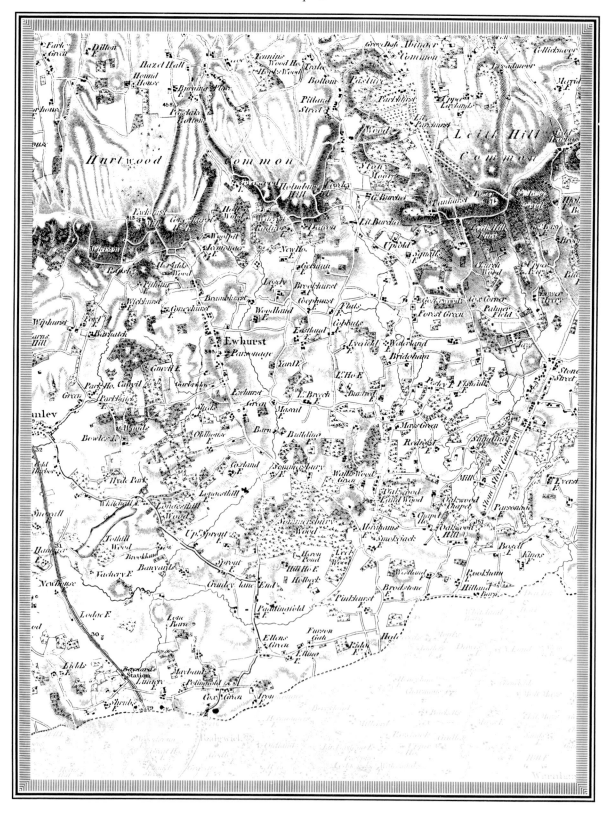

Map 22

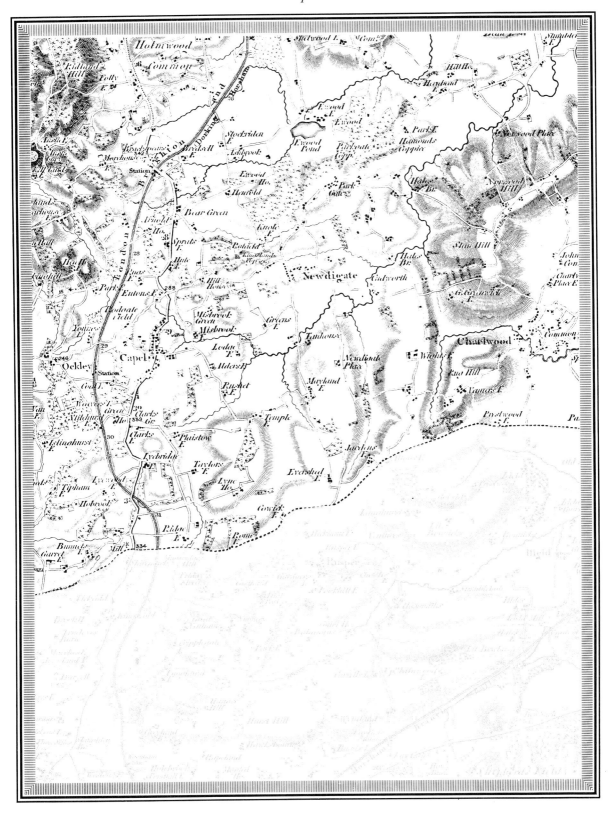

Map 21 cont.

the proceeds of an appeal sponsored by *The Times*. In 1930–31, local residents, including the composer Dr Ralph Vaughan Williams, again prevented the erection of houses on the hill.

———————◇◇◇———————

Map 22 and 23 (previous page and opposite) Fringing the central core of the High Weald is the vale of the Low Weald, and the Weald Clay is associated with heavy damp soils which Cobbett claimed 'would only grow three things well—oak trees, wheat and grass'. Field drainage has modified the traditional picture of waterlogged conditions in recent years but, seen from the southern edge of Blackdown or Leith Hill, this is still a landscape very much in the bocage mould with its well-wooded appearance and patchwork of small green fields. Woodland, mainly coppiced oak and ash, occurs in the ill-drained areas, as well as in narrow belts or 'shaws' surrounding the fields, and accounts for more than a quarter of the total land surface. The land is exceptionally flat in some parts—hence Dunsfold aerodrome (see map on page 118) and Gatwick Airport—and river gradients are very slight, often only 60cm per kilometre (3 feet per mile). Where the land is cultivated a high percentage is under permanent grass, but the pasture is often poor because the clay soil is usually deficient in lime and phosphates. Although the heavy intractable clay predominates, there are other rock types present and between Newdigate and Horne the limestone beds within the clay form a prominent ridge, with a minor scarp rising out of the general flatness of the clay vale.

Around 1800, there was a desperate gang or settlement of squatters on Holmwood Common. It is said that when even this neighbourhood became too hot for one of their number he would go for a while to Ashdown Forest—and similar refugees would move in the other direction.

In most English counties, agriculture still dominates the scene: fields and hedges, villages and churches have grown out of the rural economy. But in Surrey it is only in the Weald west of Gatwick Airport that this is really the case. Here agriculture is a living force with fine well cared for farms like that at Ockley Court.

Nevertheless, even here, no village is without its population of commuters. Buildings listed as being of architectural merit or historic interest are seldom occupied by people who earn their living from the land, apart from those held by the landowners themselves. Most of the more substantial timber-framed farm and manor houses of the Weald, picturesque with their fine gables, oriel windows, porches and vestiges of moats, were bought at the end of the nineteenth century by London merchants who converted them into 'gentlemen's residences'. By the Edwardian period it was very rare for one of the accessible oak-framed and stone-roofed farmhouses of Surrey to be still occupied by a farmer who farmed the attached land.

The development of Gatwick Airport and the growth of 'airport-related industries' have created much traffic growth and other pressures on the environment. The traffic congestion has been relieved by the construction of the M23 and M25 motorways, but the growth of industry and the need for additional housing have led to a substantial increase in the size of Horley that is not yet complete. Aircraft noise has affected people living in such villages as Burstow, Charlwood and Newdigate and, as a result of boundary changes, Gatwick Airport itself is now found in Sussex, not Surrey.

Map 23

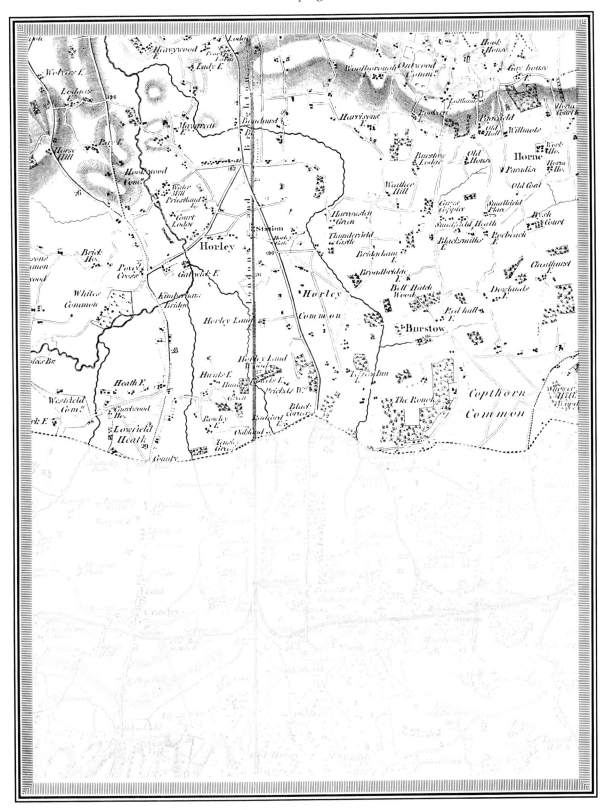

Map 24

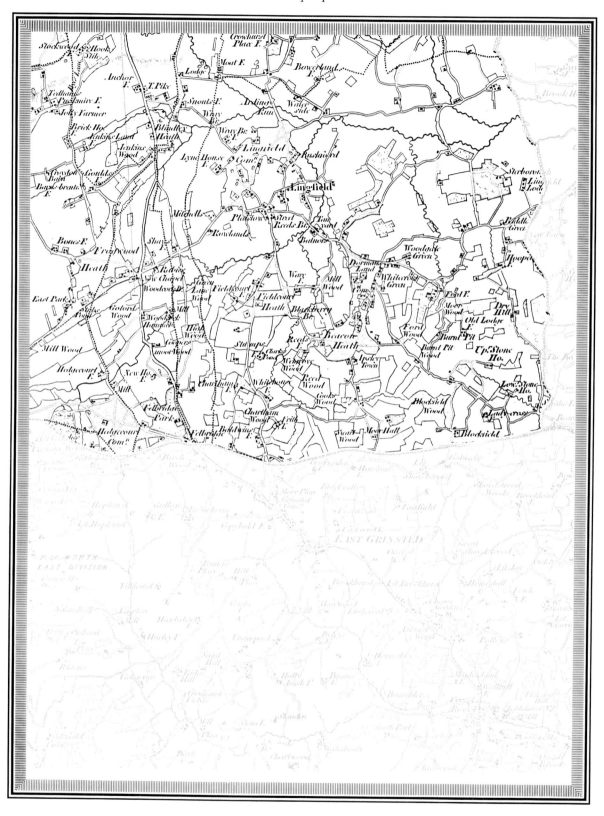

Map 25

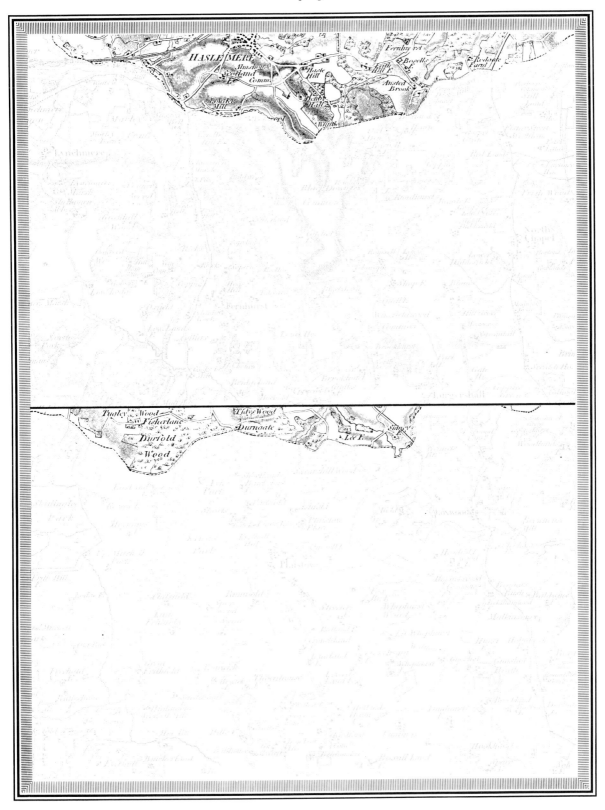

Map 24 (page 126) The ponds from the late sixteenth- and seventeenth century iron industry survive in south-east Surrey at Domewood Lake (Hedgecourt Pond) and Wire Mill Pond (by Hedgecourt Farm and Woodcock Hammer respectively). When the charcoal-burning and iron industry of the Weald had languished, agricultural production, chiefly for the London market, remained the one great staple industry of the Low Weald. In the eighteenth and nineteenth centuries, the Surrey landowner depended on farming for his rents and the small farmer also existed—but hardly flourished—in the county.

In 1809, W. Stevenson (*Review of the Agriculture of Surrey*) tells us that rents in the Weald were from 10s to less than 20s an acre: on clay land outside the Weald they were from 15s to 20s. Wages were from 13s to 15s per week on average the whole year. Prices had risen sharply since the previous century. That of wheat had doubled, from about 50s to 100s per quarter. That of beef and mutton had increased about one half. Taxation was much higher and the poor rates had soared by seven or eight times.

Today the countryside is again fast changing and land is being commercially farmed under new management principles, involving the wholesale removal of hedges and groups of trees. Hedgerows and waysides once planted with fine elms and oaks are no longer being adequately cared for. The fear is that, as Brandon put it, 'Surrey could change from a land of beauty to merely a land of beauty spots'.

Many farms on poorer ground, especially in the Weald which has always grudged a living to the small farmer, are no longer being farmed for crops but are used increasingly for 'horsey-culture'. Many of the old farmhouses have been separated from their land and have been 'gentrified' as residences for well-to-do city workers. Redundant barns are snapped up for substantial sums and converted expensively into dwellings.

Map 25 (previous page) A market was granted to the Bishop of Salisbury at Haslemere in 1220 and the town may have become a borough by 1230. The market was regranted by Elizabeth I who gave the borough the right to return two Members of Parliament. The town did not grow until the coming of the turnpike after 1758 and, more importantly, the railway in 1859. The borough lost its MPs at the 1832 Reform Act, but Haslemere is now a thriving town with a large commuter population and high house prices.

Bibliography

————◇◇◇————

Aubrey, J., *Natural History and Antiquities of Surrey* (5 vols, 1718–19; reprinted 1975)

Gover, J. E. B., Mawer, A. and Stenton, F. M., *The Place-Names of Surrey* (English Place-Names Society Volume 11, 1934; reissued 1969)

Malden, H. E., *The History of Surrey* (1900; reprinted 1977)

Manning, O. and Bray, W., *The History and Antiquities of the County of Surrey* (3 vols, 1804–14; reprinted 1974)

Nairn, L., Pevsner, N. and Cherry, B., *The Buildings of England: Surrey* (2nd edition, 1971)

Parker, E., *Surrey* (1948)

Surrey Archaeological Society, *Surrey Archaeological Collections* (vols issued approximately annually)

Surrey Local History Council, *Surrey History* (vols issued annually)

Victoria County History of Surrey (4 vols, 1908–12)

Useful Addresses

———◇◇◇———

Guildford Library (Surrey Local History Collection), North Street, Guildford

Guildford Museum, Castle Arch, Guildford

Juniper Hall Field Centre, Dorking

Kingston upon Thames Museum and Heritage Centre, Fairfield Road, Kingston upon Thames

Minet Library (Surrey Collection), 52 Knatchbull Road, London SE 5

Redhill Library (Local History Collection), Warwick Crescent, Redhill

Surrey Archaeological Society, Castle Arch, Guildford

Surrey County Record Office, County Hall, Kingston upon Thames

Surrey Domestic Buildings Research Group, 11 Lintons Lane, Epsom

Surrey Local History Council, Jenner House, 2 Jenner Road, Guildford

West Surrey Muniment Room, Castle Arch, Guildford

Weybridge Museum, Council Offices, Weybridge

Wilmer House Museum, 38 West Street, Farnham

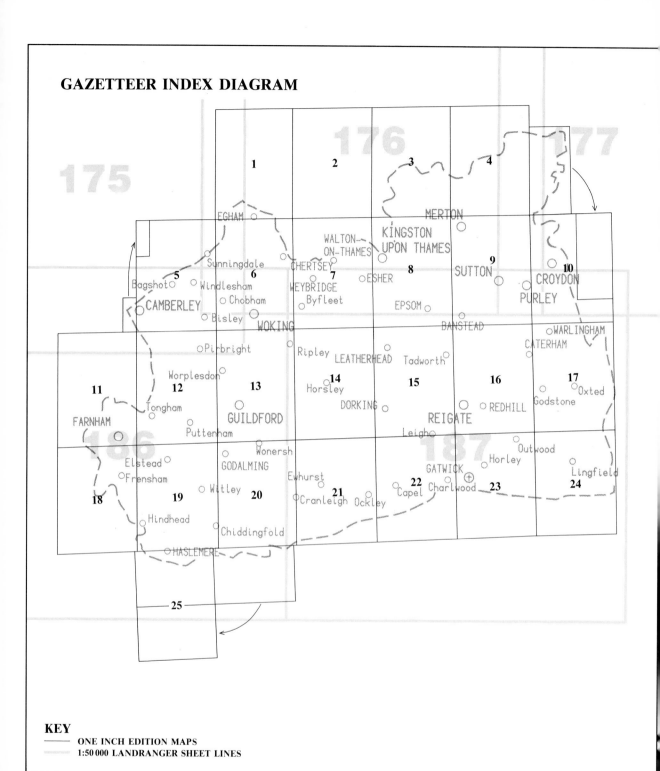

GAZETTEER INDEX DIAGRAM

1   2   3   4

175   176   177

EGHAM

MERTON

WALTON-ON-THAMES

KINGSTON UPON THAMES

Sunningdale   CHERTSEY   SUTTON   9

5   6   7   8   CROYDON   10

Bagshot   Windlesham   WEYBRIDGE   ESHER   PURLEY

CAMBERLEY   Chobham   Byfleet   EPSOM

Bisley   WOKING   BANSTEAD   WARLINGHAM

Pirbright   Ripley   LEATHERHEAD   Tadworth   CATERHAM

Worplesdon   14   15   16   17

11   12   13   Horsley   Oxted

Tongham   DORKING   REDHILL   Godstone

FARNHAM   GUILDFORD   REIGATE

186   Puttenham   187

Leigh

Wonersh   Outwood

Elstead   GODALMING   Horley

Frensham   Ewhurst   GATWICK   Lingfield

18   19   Witley   20   21   22   Charlwood   23   24

Hindhead   Cranleigh   Ockley   Capel

Chiddingfold

HASLEMERE

25

KEY

—— ONE INCH EDITION MAPS
····· 1:50 000 LANDRANGER SHEET LINES

GAZETTEER

Surrey

This Gazetteer contains the modern names of cities, towns and villages in the county of Surrey as shown on Ordnance Survey 1:50,000 scale Landranger maps. Each Gazetteer entry gives the place name, the Landranger map number(s) on which it appears and its National Grid reference number. Having identified the place name and the Landranger map number that includes it, references to the diagram on the left will show the page numbers of early Ordnance Survey mapping in this book where the name can be located. By purchasing the relevant Landranger map, the National Grid reference number also included in the Gazetteer will enable you to pinpoint the name and its position in the modern landscape precisely. Ordnance Survey Landranger maps are available from most booksellers, stationers and newsagents.

Ordnance Survey can also supply monochrome copies of a selection of early OS maps held in its Record Map Library. Enquiries on this service should be addressed to Fixed Price Services, Ordnance Survey, Romsey Road, Maybush, Southampton, SO9 4DH. Telephone Southampton (0703) 792338.

A

Abbey Mead	176	TQ0467
Abbotswood	186	TQ0051
Abinger Common	187	TQ1145
Abinger Hammer	187	TQ0947
Addington	177 187	TQ3764
Addington Palace	177 187	TQ3663
Addiscombe	176 177	TQ3466
Addlestone	176 186	TQ0464
Addlestonemoor	176	TQ0465
Albury	187	TQ0547
Albury Heath	187	TQ0646
Alfold	186	TQ0334
Alfold Crossways	186	TQ0435
Anerley	176 177	TQ3469
Artington	186	SU9947
Ash	186	SU8950
Ashford	176	TQ0671
Ash Green	186	SU9049
Ashley Park	176	TQ1065
Ashtead	187	TQ1858
Ashtead Park	187	TQ1957
Ash Vale	186	SU8952

B

Badshot Lea	186	SU8648
Bagshot	175 186	SU9163
Bagshot Heath	175 186	SU9161
Baldwins Hill	187	TQ3839
Balham	176	TQ2873
Bandonhill	176 187	TQ2964
Banstead	187	TQ2559
Barnes	176	TQ2276
Barwell	176 187	TQ1763
Battersea	176	TQ2876
Batt's Corner	186	SU8141
Beacon Hill	186	SU8736
Beare Green	187	TQ1743
Beddington	176 177	TQ3065
Beddington Corner	176	TQ2866
Bellfields	186	SU9951
Belmont	176 187	TQ2562
Benhilton	176	TQ2665
Bermondsey	176 177	TQ3379
Berrylands	176	TQ1967
Betchworth	187	TQ2150
Binscombe	186	SU9645
Bishopsgate	175 176	SU9871
Bisley	175 186	SU9559
Bisley Camp	175 186	SU9357
Blackbrook	187	TQ1846
Bletchingley	187	TQ3350
Blindley Heath	187	TQ3645
Boundstone	186	SU8344
Bourne, The	186	SU8444
Bowlhead Green	186	SU9138
Box Hill	187	TQ1951
Bramley	186	TQ0044
Brewer Street	187	TQ3251
Brick Hill	175 176	
	186	SU9564
Bridge End	187	TQ0757
Brixton	176 177	TQ3175

C

Broadford	186	SU9946
Broad Green	176 177	TQ3266
Broadham Green	187	TQ3851
Broadmoor	187	TQ1345
Brockham	187	TQ1949
Brook	186	SU9337
Brook	187	TQ0646
Brooklands	176 187	TQ0662
Brook Place	175 176	
	186	SU9561
Brookwood	175 186	SU9557
Broomfields	186	SU8342
Broomhall	175 176	SU9566
Buckland	187	TQ2250
Bullswater Common	186	SU9554
Bunce Common	187	TQ2046
Burgh Heath	187	TQ2457
Burntcommon	186	TQ0354
Burpham	186	TQ0152
Burrowhill	175 176	
	186	SU9763
Burrows Cross	187	TQ0846
Burstow	187	TQ3041
Burwood Park	176 187	TQ1064
Busbridge	186	SU9742
Bushbury	187	TQ1947
Bushey Mead	176	TQ2368
Bushy Hill	186	TQ0251
Byfleet	176 187	TQ0661

Camberley	175 186	SU8860
Camberwell	176 177	TQ3377
Capel	187	TQ1740
Carshalton	176 187	TQ2764
Carshalton Beeches	176 187	TQ2763
Carshalton on the Hill	176 187	TQ2863
Cartbridge	186	TQ0156
Castle Green	175 176	
	186	SU9660
Caterham	187	TQ3355
Catteshall	186	SU9844
Chaldon	187	TQ3155
Charleshill	186	SU8944
Charlwood	187	TQ2441
Cheam	176 187	TQ2462
Chelsham	187	TQ3759
Chertsey	176	TQ0466
Chertsey Meads	176	TQ0566
Chessington	176 187	TQ1863
Chiddingfold	186	SU9535
Chilworth	186	TQ0247
Chipstead	187	TQ2757
Chobham	175 176	
	186	SU9761
Christmaspie	186	SU9249
Church End	187	TQ0656
Church Town	187	TQ3551
Churt	186	SU8538
Clapham	176	TQ2975
Clapham Park	176	TQ2974
Clark's Green	187	TQ1739
Claygate	176 187	TQ1663
Clock House	176 187	TQ2860
Cobham	176 187	TQ1160
Coldharbour	187	TQ1443
Coles Meads	187	TQ2751
Collier's Wood	176	TQ2770
Combe Common	186	SU9535

Compton	186	SU8546
Compton	186	SU9546
Coombe	176	TQ2070
Cooper's Hill	175 176	SU9972
Copse Hill	176	TQ2270
Copthorne	187	TQ3139
Cottenham Park	176	TQ2269
Coulsdon	187	TQ3058
Cox Green	187	TQ0934
Cramhurst	186	SU9440
Cranleigh	187	TQ0638
Crawley Hill	175 186	SU8860
Critchmere	186	SU8833
Crosswater	186	SU8539
Crossways	186	SU8538
Crowhurst	187	TQ3947
Crowhurst Lane End	187	TQ3748
Crownpits	186	SU9743
Croydon	176 177	
	187	TQ3364
Croydon	176 177	TQ3365
Cuckoo Hill	175 186	SU9360
Cudworth	187	TQ2141
Culmer	186	SU9439

D

Dawesgreen	187	TQ2147
Dawney's Hill	175 186	SU9456
Deepcut	175 186	SU9057
Deepdene	187	TQ1749
Deptford	177	TQ3677
Dippenhall	186	SU8146
Dockenfield	186	SU8240
Domewood	187	TQ3440
Donkey Town	175 186	SU9360
Dorking	187	TQ1649
Dormansland	187	TQ4042
Dormans Park	187	TQ3940
Doversgreen	187	TQ2548
Downside	187	TQ1058
Downside	187	TQ1755
Downs, The	186	SU9535
Dulwich	176 177	TQ3472
Dulwich Village	176 177	TQ3373
Dunsfold Common	186	TQ0035
Dunsfold Green	186	TQ0036
Dunsford	186	TQ0036

E

Earlsfield	176	TQ2673
Earlswood	187	TQ2849
Eashing	186	SU9443
East Clandon	187	TQ0551
East Dulwich	176 177	TQ3474
East Ewell	176 187	TQ2362
East Horsley	187	TQ0953
East Molesey	176	TQ1467
East Sheen	176	TQ2075
Edgeborough	186	SU8443
Effingham	187	TQ1153
Effingham Common	187	TQ1055
Egham	176	TQ0071
Egham Wick	175 176	SU9870
Ellen's Green	187	TQ0935
Elm Corner	187	TQ0757
Elstead	186	SU9043
Englefield Green	175 176	SU9971

Place	Map	Grid
Enton Green	186	SU9540
Epsom	176 187	TQ2060
Esher	176 187	TQ1464
Ewell	176 187	TQ2162
Ewhurst	187	TQ0940
Ewhurst Green	187	TQ0939

F

Place	Map	Grid
Fairlands	186	SU9652
Fairmile	176 187	TQ1161
Farindons	187	TQ4041
Farleigh	177 187	TQ3760
Farleigh Court	177 187	TQ3760
Farley Green	187	TQ0645
Farncombe	186	SU9745
Farnham	186	SU8446
Felbridge	187	TQ3639
Felcourt	187	TQ3841
Fernhill	187	TQ3041
Fetcham	187	TQ1455
Fickleshole	177 187	TQ3860
Field Common	176	TQ1266
Flexford	186	SU9250
Forestdale	177 187	TQ3662
Forest Green	187	TQ1241
Fox Corner	186	SU9654
Fredley	187	TQ1652
Frensham	186	SU8441
Friday Street	187	TQ1245
Frimley	175 186	SU8858
Frimley Green	175 186	SU8856
Frimley Ridge	175 186	SU8959
Frith Hill	186	SU9644
Furzedown	176	TQ2870

G

Place	Map	Grid
Gadbrook	187	TQ2047
Gatton	187	TQ2753
Gatwick	186	SU9144
Giggshill	176	TQ1666
Givons Grove	187	TQ1754
Godalming	186	SU9643
Godstone	187	TQ3551
Gomshall	187	TQ0847
Grafham	186	TQ0241
Gravelpit Hill	186	SU9051
Grayswood	186	SU9134
Grayswood Common	186	SU9134
Great Bookham	187	TQ1354
Great Burgh	187	TQ2358
Great Enton	186	SU9539
Green Cross	186	SU8638
Guildford	186	SU9949
Guildford Park	186	SU9849

H

Place	Map	Grid
Hackbridge	176	TQ2865
Hale	186	SU8448
Ham	176	TQ1772
Hambledon	186	SU9638
Hamm Moor	176 187	TQ0664
Hamsey Green	187	TQ3559
Hascombe	186	TQ0039
Haslemere	186	SU8932
Hatton Hill	175 186	SU9364
Hawk's Hill	187	TQ1555
Haxted	187	TQ4245
Headley	187	TQ2054
Heath End	186	SU8449
Heathfield	177 187	TQ3563
Herne Hill	176 177	TQ3274
Hersham	176 187	TQ1164
High Curley	175 186	SU9161
Hinchley Wood	176	TQ1565
Hindhead	186	SU8836
Hoe Place	186	TQ0257
Hog Hatch	186	SU8348
Holland	187	TQ4050
Holloway Hill	186	SU9742
Holmbury St Mary	187	TQ1144
Honor Oak	177	TQ3574
Hook	176 187	TQ1864
Hook Heath	175 186	SU9857
Hookwood	187	TQ2642
Hooley	187	TQ2856
Horley	187	TQ2843
Horne	187	TQ3344
Horsell	175 186	SU9959
Horsell Birch	175 186	SU9859
Howell Hill	176 187	TQ2362
Hurst Green	187	TQ3951
Hurst Park	176	TQ1368
Hurtmore	186	SU9545
Hydestile	186	SU9640
Hythe	176	TQ0270

I

Place	Map	Grid
Irons Bottom	187	TQ2546

J

Place	Map	Grid
Jacobs Well	186	SU9952

K

Place	Map	Grid
Kenley	187	TQ3259
Kennington	176 177	TQ3077
Kew	176	TQ1977
Kingfield	186	TQ0057
Kingston Upon Thames	176	TQ1870
Kingston Vale	176	TQ2171
Kingswood	187	TQ2456
Kingswood Warren	187	TQ2455
Knaphill	175 186	SU9658
Knight's Hill	176 177	TQ3273
Knowle Hill	175 176	SU9866

L

Place	Map	Grid
Laker's Green	186	TQ0335
Lambeth	176 177	TQ3078
Lane End	186	SU8441
Langley Vale	187	TQ2157
Leatherhead	187	TQ1656
Leatherhead Common	187	TQ1558
Leigh	187	TQ2246
Lightwater	175 186	SU9262
Limpsfield	187	TQ3953
Limpsfield Chart	187	TQ4251
Limpsfield Common	187	TQ4152
Lingfield	187	TQ3843
Lingfield Common	187	TQ3844
Little Bookham	187	TQ1254
Littlefield Common	186	SU9552
Little Heath	176 187	TQ1360
Little Tangley	186	TQ0246
Littleton	186	SU9847
Little Woodcote	176 187	TQ2861
Longcross	175 176	SU9865
Long Ditton	176	TQ1666
Lordshill Common	186	TQ0243
Lower Ashtead	187	TQ1757
Lower Bourne	186	SU8444
Lower Green	176	TQ1366
Lower Kingswood	187	TQ2453
Lowfield Heath	187	TQ2740
Loxhill	186	TQ0038
Lyne	176	TQ0166
Lythe Hill	186	SU9232

M

Place	Map	Grid
Malden Rushett	176 187	TQ1761
Margery	187	TQ2552
Martyr's Green	187	TQ0957
Maybury	186	TQ0158
Mayes Green	187	TQ1239
Mayford	175 186	SU9956
May's Green	187	TQ0957
Mead Vale	187	TQ2644
Meath Green	187	TQ2744
Merle Common	187	TQ4049
Merrow	186	TQ0250
Merstham	187	TQ2953
Merton	176	TQ2569
Merton Park	176	TQ2569
Mickleham	187	TQ1753
Middle Bourne	186	SU8444
Mid Holmwood	187	TQ1646
Milford	186	SU9442
Millbridge	186	SU8442
Mimbridge	175 176 186	SU9861
Mitcham	176	TQ2868
Mogador	187	TQ2352
Monks Orchard	177	TQ3567
Moor Park	186	SU8646
Morden	176	TQ2568
Morden Park	176	TQ2366
Mortlake	176	TQ2075
Motspur Park	176	TQ2167
Mount Hermon	186	TQ0057
Mousehill	186	SU9441
Mugswell	187	TQ2654
Mytchett	175 186	SU8855
Mytchett Place	186	SU8954

N

Place	Map	Grid
Nalderswood	187	TQ2345
Nanhurst	186	TQ0338
New Addington	177 187	TQ3862
Newchapel	187	TQ3642
New Cross	177	TQ3676
New Cross Gate	177	TQ3576
Newdigate	187	TQ1942
New Haw	176 187	TQ0563
Newington	176 177	TQ3279
Newlands Corner	186	TQ0449
New Malden	176	TQ2168
Nine Elms	176	TQ2977
Norbiton	176	TQ1969
Norbury	176 177	TQ3169
Nork	187	TQ2359
Norley Common	186	TQ0244
Normandy	186	SU9251
Norney	186	SU9444
North Cheam	176	TQ2465
North Holmwood	187	TQ1647
North Looe	176 187	TQ2260
North Sheen	176	TQ1976
Norwood Hill	187	TQ2443
Norwood New Town	176 177	TQ3270
Nunhead	177	TQ3575
Nutcombe	186	SU8834
Nutfield	187	TQ3050

O

Place	Map	Grid
Oaklands	187	TQ0538
Oaks, The	175 176 186	SU9560
Oakwoodhill	187	TQ1337
Oatlands Park	176 187	TQ0964
Ockford Ridge	186	SU9542
Ockham	187	TQ0756
Ockley	187	TQ1440
Old Coulsdon	187	TQ3157
Old Malden	176	TQ2166
Old Woking	186	TQ0157
Onslow Village	186	SU9749
Ottershaw	176 186	TQ0263
Outwood	187	TQ3245
Oxshott	176 187	TQ1460
Oxted	187	TQ3852

P

Place	Map	Grid
Pains Hill	187	TQ4151
Palmers Cross	186	TQ0240
Park Barn	186	SU9750
Parkgate	187	TQ2043
Peaslake	187	TQ0844
Peasmarsh	186	SU9946
Pebble Coombe	187	TQ2152
Peckham	176 177	TQ3476
Penge	176 177	TQ3470
Penton Hook	176	TQ0469
Peper Harow	186	SU9344
Petersham	176	TQ1773
Pirbright	175 186	SU9455
Pirbright Camp	175 186	SU9256
Pitch Place	186	SU8939
Pitch Place	186	SU9752
Pixham	187	TQ1750
Pot Common	186	SU9042
Povey Cross	187	TQ2642
Prey Heath	175 186	SU9955
Purley	176 177 187	TQ3161
Putney	176	TQ2375
Putney Heath	176	TQ2373
Putney Vale	176	TQ2272
Puttenham	186	SU9347
Pyle Hill	175 186	SU9955
Pyrford	186	TQ0359
Pyrford Common	186	TQ0359

Place	Sheet	Grid
Pyrford Green	186	TQ0458
Pyrford Village	186	TQ0458

R

Place	Sheet	Grid
Ramsnest Common	186	SU9433
Ranmore Common	187	TQ1450
Raynes Park	176	TQ2368
Red Court	186	SU9032
Redhill	187	TQ2750
Reigate	187	TQ2649
Reigate Heath	187	TQ2350
Richmond	176	TQ1874
Ridge Green	187	TQ3048
Ridgway	186	TQ0459
Ripley	187	TQ0556
Roehampton	176	TQ2274
Rosehill	176	TQ2666
Rose Hill	187	TQ1649
Rotherhithe	177	TQ3579
Roundshaw	176 177 187	TQ3063
Rowhill	176 186	TQ0363
Rowledge	186	SU8243
Rowly	186	TQ0440
Row Town	176 186	TQ0463
Runfold	186	SU8747
Rushett Common	186	TQ0242
Rushmoor	186	SU8740
Russell Hill	176 177 187	TQ3061
Russ Hill	187	TQ2340

S

Place	Sheet	Grid
St George's Hill	176 187	TQ0762
St Helier	176	TQ2766
St Johns	175 186	SU9857
Salfords	187	TQ2846
Sanderstead	176 177 187	TQ3361
Sandgates	176	TQ0365
Sandhills	186	SU9337
Sands, The	186	SU8846
Sandy Cross	186	SU8847
Scilly Isles, The	176	TQ1565
Seale	186	SU8947
Selhurst	176 177	TQ3267
Selsdon	177 187	TQ3562
Send	186	TQ0255
Send Grove	186	TQ0154
Send Marsh	186	TQ0355
Shackleford	186	SU9345
Shalford	186	TQ0046
Shamley Green	186	TQ0243
Sheerwater	176 186	TQ0260
Sheets Heath	175 186	SU9457
Shere	187	TQ0747
Shipley Bridge	187	TQ3040
Shirley	177	TQ3566
Shortfield Common	186	SU8442
Shortheath	186	SU8244
Shottermill	186	SU8832
Shrubs Hill	175 176	SU9667
Sidlow	187	TQ2546
Silverlands	176	TQ0165
Slyfield	186	SU9952
Smallbrook	186	SU8939
Smallfield	187	TQ3143

Place	Sheet	Grid
South Beddington	176 187	TQ2963
Southborough	176	TQ1866
South Croydon	176 177 187	TQ3263
Southfields	176	TQ2573
South Godstone	187	TQ3547
South Holmwood	187	TQ1745
South Lambeth	176 177	TQ3076
South Mersham	187	TQ2952
South Norwood	176 177	TQ3368
South Nutfield	187	TQ3049
South Park	187	TQ2448
South Wimbledon	176	TQ2570
Spreakley	186	SU8441
Spring Park	177	TQ3665
Stanners Hill	175 176 186	SU9963
Stockwell	176 177	TQ3075
Stoke D' Abernon	187	TQ1259
Stonebridge	187	TQ1747
Stoneleigh	176 187	TQ2264
Stoughton	186	SU9851
Streatham	176 177	TQ3071
Streatham Hill	176 177	TQ3073
Streatham Park	176	TQ2971
Streatham Vale	176	TQ2970
Strood Green	187	TQ2048
Stroud Common	186	TQ0342
Stroude	176	TQ0068
Summerstown	176	TQ2672
Surbiton	176	TQ1767
Sutton	176 187	TQ2564
Sutton	187	TQ1045
Sutton Green	186	TQ0054
Sydenhurst	186	SU9534

T

Place	Sheet	Grid
Tadworth	187	TQ2256
Thames Ditton	176	TQ1567
The Borough	176 177	TQ3279
The Wells	176 187	TQ1960
The Wrythe	176	TQ2765
Thorncombe Street	186	SU9942
Thornton Heath	176 177	TQ3168
Thorpe	176	TQ0168
Thorpe Green	176	TQ0168
Thorpe Lea	176	TQ0270
Thursley	186	SU9039
Tilford	186	SU8743
Tilford Common	186	SU8742
Tinsley Green	187	TQ2839
Titsey	187	TQ4054
Tolworth	176	TQ1965
Tongham	186	SU8849
Tooting Graveney	176	TQ2771
Tower Hill	187	TQ1648
Trumps Green	175 176	SU9967
Truxford	186	SU8940
Tuesley	186	SU9641
Tulse Hill	176 177	TQ3173
Tyler's Green	187	TQ3552
Tyrrells Wood	187	TQ1855

U

Place	Sheet	Grid
Upper Eashing	186	SU9543
Upper Hale	186	SU8449

Place	Sheet	Grid
Upper Ifold	186	TQ0033
Upper Norwood	176 177	TQ3369
Upper Shirley	177 187	TQ3564
Upper Tooting	176	TQ2772

V

Place	Sheet	Grid
Vauxhall	176 177	TQ3078
Virginia Water	175 176	SU9967

W

Place	Sheet	Grid
Waddon	176 177 187	TQ3164
Wallington	176 187	TQ2964
Walliswood	187	TQ1138
Walton-on-Thames	176	TQ1066
Walton on the Hill	187	TQ2254
Walworth	176 177	TQ3278
Wanborough	186	SU9348
Wandle Park	176 177	TQ3165
Wandsworth	176	TQ2575
Warlingham	187	TQ3558
Warwick Wold	187	TQ3152
Waterside	187	TQ3945
Weatherhill	187	TQ3143
West Barnes	176	TQ2267
Westbrook	186	SU9643
West Byfleet	176 186	TQ0460
West Clandon	186	TQ0452
Westcott	187	TQ1448
West Dulwich	176 177	TQ3272
West End	186	SU8242
West End	175 186	SU9460
West End	176 187	TQ1263
West Ewell	176 187	TQ2063
Westfield	186	TQ0056
West Hill	176	TQ2474
West Horsley	187	TQ0752
Westhumble	187	TQ1651
West Molesey	176	TQ1368
West Norwood	176 177	TQ3271
Weston Green	176	TQ1566
Weybourne	186	SU8549
Weybridge	176 187	TQ0864
Weydown Common	186	SU9034
Wheelerstreet	186	SU9440
Whiteley Village	176 187	TQ0962
Whitfield Court	175 186	SU9659
Whyteleafe	187	TQ3358
Willey Green	186	SU9351
Wimbledon	176	TQ2471
Windlesham	175 186	SU9363
Wisley	187	TQ0659
Witley	186	SU9439
Woking	186	TQ0058
Woldingham	187	TQ3756
Woldingham Garden Village	187	TQ3656
Wonersh	186	TQ0145
Wonersh Common	186	TQ0246
Woodbridge Hill	186	SU9850
Woodcote	176 177 187	TQ3061
Woodcote	187	TQ2059
Woodcote Green	176 187	TQ2962
Wood Field	187	TQ1759
Woodham	176 186	TQ0462
Woodhatch	187	TQ2548

Place	Sheet	Grid
Woodmansterne	187	TQ2759
Woodside	176 177	TQ3467
Wood Street	186	SU9550
Worcester Park	176	TQ2265
Wormley	186	SU9438
Worplesdon	186	SU9753
Wotton	187	TQ1247
Wray Common	187	TQ2650
Wrecclesham	186	SU8244
Wyke	186	SU9251

Y

Place	Sheet	Grid
York Town	175 186	SU8659

OXFAM

VAT 348 4542 38

Oxfam's Online Shop
Shop for fashion, homeware,
books, music and more

www.oxfam.org.uk/shop

CK   SALES   F4221/POS1
NDAY 13 AUGUST 2017   12:08 041539
    GIFT AID 20112247554221
NON FICTION   £1.99

           1 Items
TOTAL   **£1.99**
CASH   £2.00
CHANGE   £0.01
    Oxfam Shop: F4221
     32, High Street,
    Godalming, GU7 1DZ
      01483 424441
    oxfam.org.uk/shop